T. W. HENDRICK, FRSA
Maps by the author

Discovering
Walks in West Sussex

SHIRE PUBLICATIONS LTD

ACKNOWLEDGEMENTS

Acknowledgements are made to the Editor and the proprietors of the *West Sussex Gazette* who, at the instigation of the Arundel Society, published in a series of fortnightly articles the walks described in this book; the thanks of the author and publishers are due to them for their kind permission to reproduce the articles and maps.

The Rights of Way Department of West Sussex County Council were most helpful in checking the routes and all walkers and riders in West Sussex will appreciate the considerable amount of organisation and effort on the part of the County Council in siting, providing and erecting the numerous hardwood fingerposts that guide the way along the footpaths and bridleways throughout the county.

Thanks are particularly due to the Society of Sussex Downsmen and the Sussex Rights of Way Group, whose continual vigilance helps to ensure that the rights of way and amenities are preserved for the use of the public; the latter group also organises voluntary working parties who help to keep the paths clear until such time as the County Council can assume responsibility for this essential work. The Ramblers' Association, too, has played no small part in path clearance.

 No. 217 in the 'Discovering' series. ISBN 0 85263 342 4. First published 1976; reprinted 1980.

Printed in Great Britain by City Print (Milton Keynes) Ltd,
16 Denbigh Hall, Bletchley, Milton Keynes, MK3 7QT

Contents

Introduction

The twenty walks described in this booklet have been selected from a series of articles covering the southern area of West Sussex and, since the downland walks generally provide the greatest interest, the routes range from Harting, on the borders of Hampshire, eastward along the South Downs Way to the Devil's Dyke, near Brighton.

The distances covered range from six to ten miles so that the routes can be selected to suit the physical capacity of the walker and his family but, in each case, the directions bring

The asterisks show the starting points of each of the twenty walks in this book.

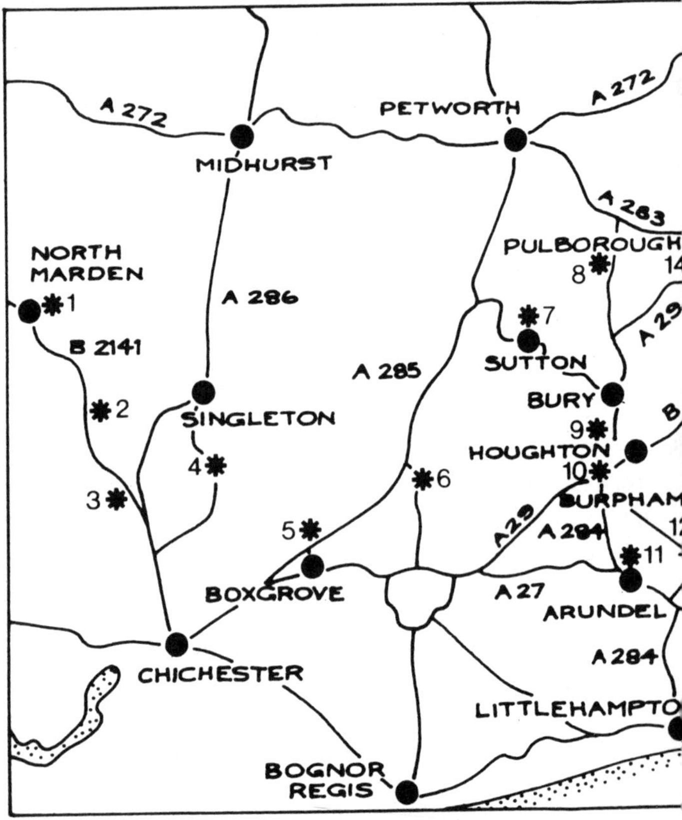

him back to the point from whence he started. Apart from the obvious convenience of this arrangement, it avoids the need to make connections with different routes of public transport which, alas, seem to become scarcer and more unreliable each year.

A 'definitive' (master) map showing the legal rights of way along footpaths, bridleways and byways is kept up to date at the offices of the West Sussex County Council at Chichester; this map should, if possible, be consulted before starting on any walks. Although the routes in this book were checked before going to press, official diversions are likely to have

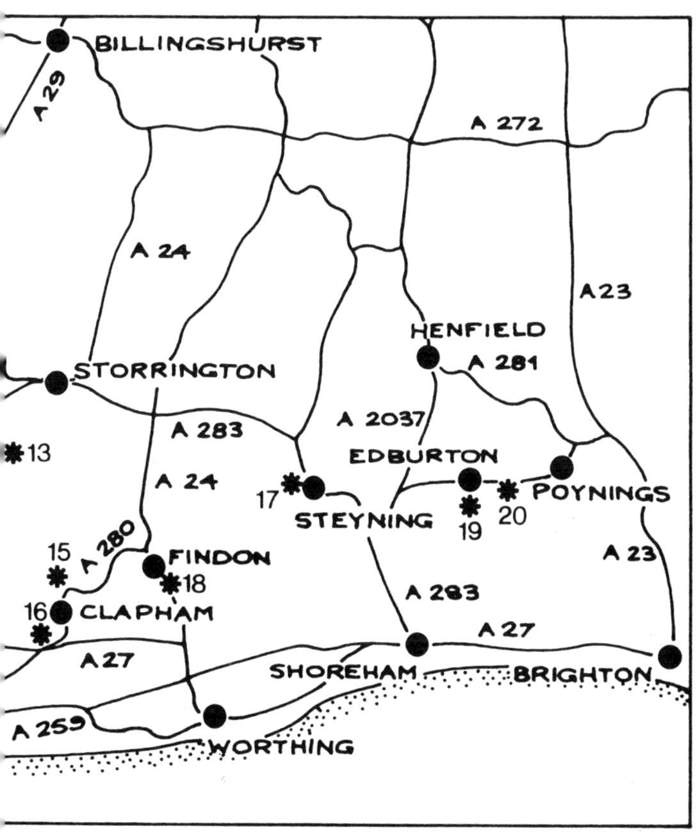

been made in the meantime. However, whenever such a diversion is made, an alternative route is described and posted up at the point of diversion and there is generally little variation in the distance to be covered.

Finally, do make sure to observe the Country Code: avoid trespassing on private property; keep to the specified rights of way; shut all gates behind you; light no fires; leave no litter; do not disturb cattle or sheep and keep dogs on a lead when passing near livestock and game preserves.

The maps

The sketch-maps are not drawn to scale – since this might infringe Crown copyright. In consequence, the distances shown between various points on the routes are not always proportionate to a precise degree.

Walkers are therefore strongly urged to provide themselves with the 1: 25,000 scale (approximately 2½ inches to the mile) Ordnance Survey maps mentioned in the text; not many of these are required since the same maps cover a number of walks. This scale provides details which are essential and not always shown on one-inch scale maps, but bear in mind that public paths shown on the Ordnance Survey sheet do not take into account any diversions made by the County Council after the maps were printed.

Do provide yourself with a pocket compass, because compass directions are given in the text and, in any case, it makes any walk more interesting when, like a true 'discoverer', you have to set your course and check it.

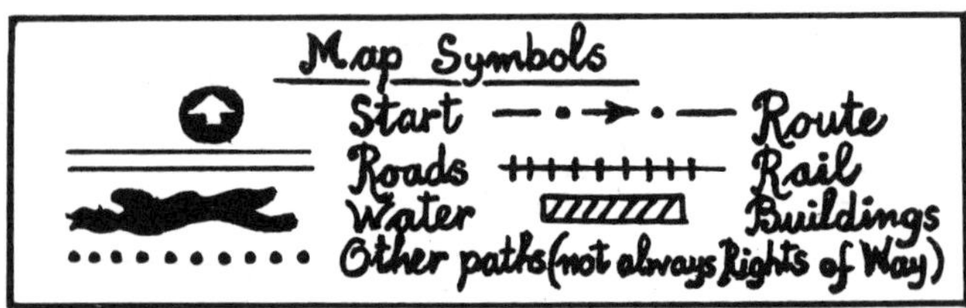

1. Over Harting Downs

This walk over the Downs covers nearly six miles; the route is shown on OS map sheets SU71 and SU81. The entire walk should take about three hours – allowing for rests; dogs must be kept on a lead near private property and livestock.

About halfway between Chilgrove and South Harting, going westward on B2141, there is a turning going south-west to North Marden, but about two hundred yards before you reach it you will see a fingerpost pointing to a path on the right. Go through an iron gateway and north-east up this narrow, overhung green path between the hedges.

Less than half a mile on, the path opens out on to fields, with the variegated afforestation of Germanleith Copse to the east. Pause here – this is a meeting of the ways – then take the path going north towards the copper beeches. After passing a group of buildings on the left you will come out on to a hard, private road that leads north between the avenue of beeches towards Beacon Hill House; the way is well signposted to prevent trespassing.

Carry on, due north, along the road, passing Beacon Hill House on your left, and then ahead on to a pathway. Soon you will arrive at a fork in the path and will note that here is an exceptionally acute angle in the line of the South Downs Way – the path comes down from the north-north-east and turns north-north-west. Take the latter, left-hand fork.

After crossing some scrubland the path opens out on to a wonderful vista of downland scenery. On your right, across Millpond Bottom, is Pen Hill; to the left you see Little Round Down sloping to the impressively steep depths of Bramshott Bottom, and ahead is a grand view of Beacon Hill, nearly eight hundred feet high; the prehistoric fort and ramparts on the summit, clearly, commanded a very strategic position.

Your way lies along the western side of the hill, with the deep green valley on your left. At the edge of the escarpment of the Downs you come to a ruggedly strong and stout signpost erected on a stone cairn by the Society of Sussex Downsmen in 1971. This multi-arm post points five ways: north to East Harting; east to Treyford; south (your approach); south-west towards Compton; and westward – the way you want to go. But before leaving this spot take a good look at the steeply banked sheep walk going down to East Harting. Lined with thorn bushes, this little green gap in the hills is typical of the original, unchanged downland scene.

Carry on westward up the gentle slope to Harting Hill. This is a particularly enjoyable stretch of the South Downs Way – open and free – with grand views of the Weald northward to

East Harting, South Harting, Rogate, and Trotton, and ahead of you, to the west, you will see the ruined building high on Tower Hill, in Uppark.

Eventually you arrive at a clearing where cars are parked. Turn sharp left here and follow the narrow path winding through the trees; you will hear the roar of the traffic on

Walk 1

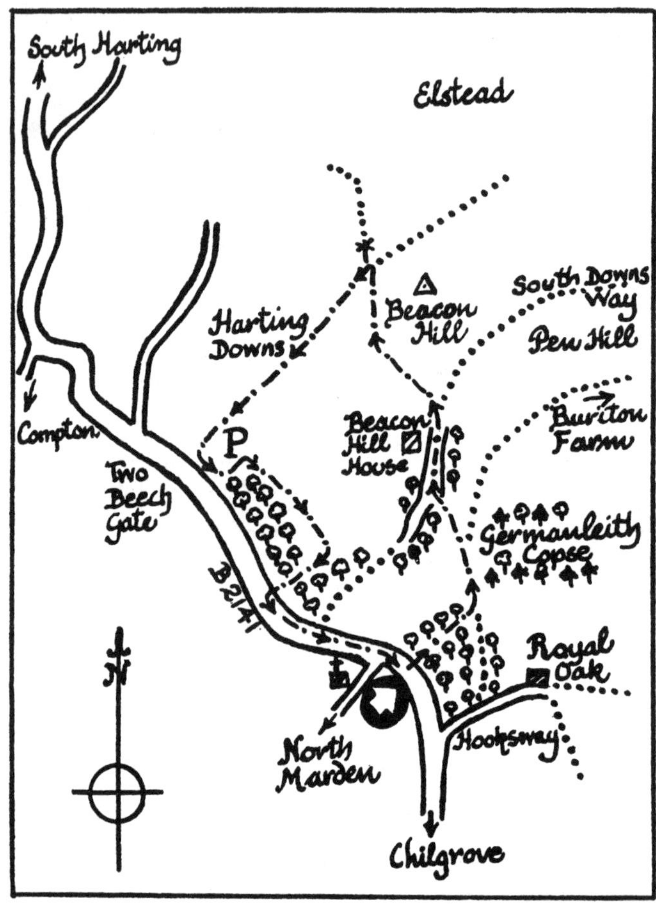

Harting Hill close on your right, but soon you come to a clearing and bear left, away from it.

The path takes you around the eastern side of the trees skirting Whitcombe Bottom and then you arrive at Kill Devil Copse – and a T junction in the path; turn sharp right here and then left, along the B2141 road.

The walks in this book are planned to bring you back to your starting point and, to avoid retracing your steps for part of the way, it is sometimes necessary to finish up on a main road. However, it is only about a mile back to the North Marden signpost – and the road has wide grass verges.

---

2. Westdean Woods, Cocking and Treyford

The following route covers approximately ten miles and is shown on OS map sheet SU81. A dog would have to be kept on the lead most of the way.

About three miles along the road from Lavant (B2141) that passes Kingley Vale and Bow Hill, on its way to Harting, you come to Brick Kiln Farm, on the right. Follow the narrow road, Hylters Lane, that goes due north-east for about two miles; then the lane intersects with the road to West Dean.

At this point a wide path continues north-east, with Westdean Woods on the left and the arable land of Colworth Down on the right. As you walk up the gentle ascent you will notice piles of pit-props and other signs of intensive forestry operations in the woods. When the path enters the trees it becomes a slightly steeper climb and bears north, with Venus Wood to the west and Stubbs Copse to the east; keep to the public path all the way – the woods are private.

Following the fingerposts pointing in a northerly direction you will skirt the western end of Warren Bottom and emerge through the plantations of young trees at Cocking Down – on the South Downs Way. Here you have a grand view of Heyshott Down to the east and Cobden's village of Cocking nestling below it, with the Weald spreading out to the north.

After the effort of climbing to the crest of the hills, the pleasure of striding west along the smooth and level South Downs Way is particularly enjoyable; the woods are beautiful but their very density can, after a while, prove somewhat oppressive. By comparison, the 'Way' is clear and open and always creates an atmosphere of euphoria.

There are splendid views on all sides. To the north, a great

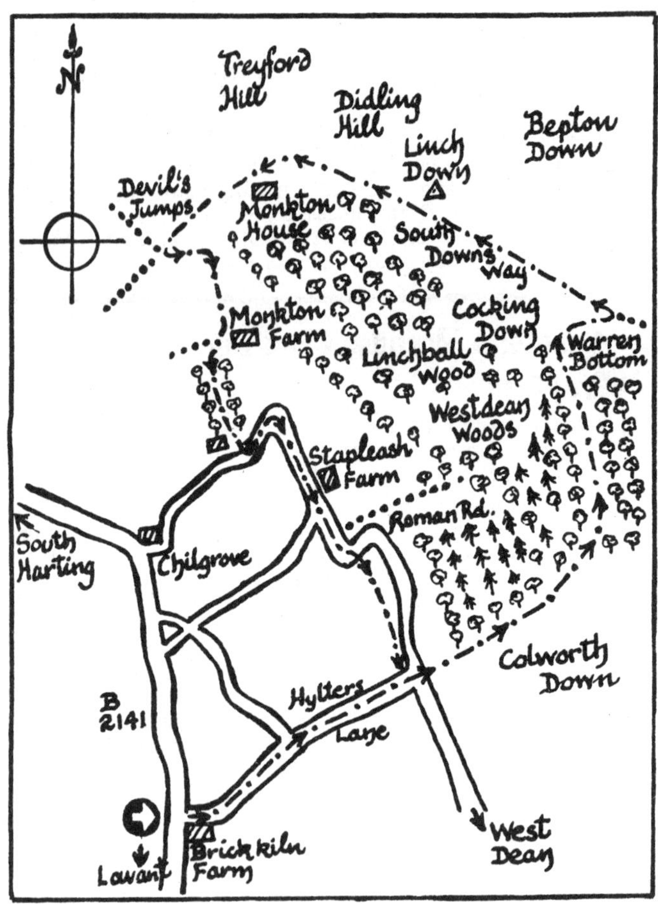

Walk 2

expanse of the Weald is revealed: you can see Midhurst in the distance and, beyond it, the heights of Blackdown near Haslemere. To the west the curving line of the Downs goes on to Harting, Buriton and beyond. Southwards, above the treetops of the dense forests, you will see the foothills rolling down to the coastal plain.

The broad track crosses Bepton Down and Linch Down –

with its triangulation station at 813 feet. Carry on over Didling Hill to Treyford Hill, capped with scrubland; on your left is the close wire fence enclosing the grounds and gardens of Monkton House with its clock-tower and, although you may not see them, you will probably hear the loud and strange cries of the exotic birds in the aviary.

Past the wire fence, on the right, are five tumuli, known as the Devil's Jumps; the fields slope down to the left and soon you come to a four-way fingerpost. Leaving the South Downs Way, turn left, through a gate, on to a path; this leads downhill to the low buildings of Monkton Farm. Here another fingerpost points straight on, through a gate, and slightly uphill. The path winds its way through a tree-tunnel spinney for about a mile and then emerges into the open; a flint cottage is on the left and a pair of houses – Yew Tree Cottages – on your right; then you come to the Chilgrove road.

Turn left here and follow the road past Stapleash Farm to the sharp bend on the hill; you will cross over the line of a Roman Road and will easily discern the raised bank, or agger, leading north-east. At the bend of the road is a fingerpost pointing to a path leading south-east for about half a mile – then you arrive back at the point where you entered the path that goes past Westdean Woods.

---

3. Kingley Vale and Bow Hill

This visit to the nature reserve comprises a six-mile walk and the route is shown on OS maps SU80 and SU81. No dogs are allowed on the reserve.

You can set off from Chichester – straight up North Street until you come to Mid Lavant. Keep on the main road (A286) through the village until you reach the B2141 forking off to the left towards Chilgrove.

About a quarter of a mile up this road, on the left, you will come to Welldown Farm – a pleasant example of Sussex flint building, with the lichen gilding its red-tiled roof. Here a fingerpost indicates a path leading west. There is ample room for parking on the wide grass verge of B2141.

Follow the path (or flint cart track) up a gentle slope; looking back, you can see The Trundle at Goodwood. The track curves up, skirting Welldown Copse, and then the view opens out on to rolling arable land. Far to the south the spire of Chichester cathedral can be seen and to the north the long range of downland that is Bow Hill.

Looking ahead, you will see the dense, dark green foliage of the yew trees in Kingley Vale; they are said to have been

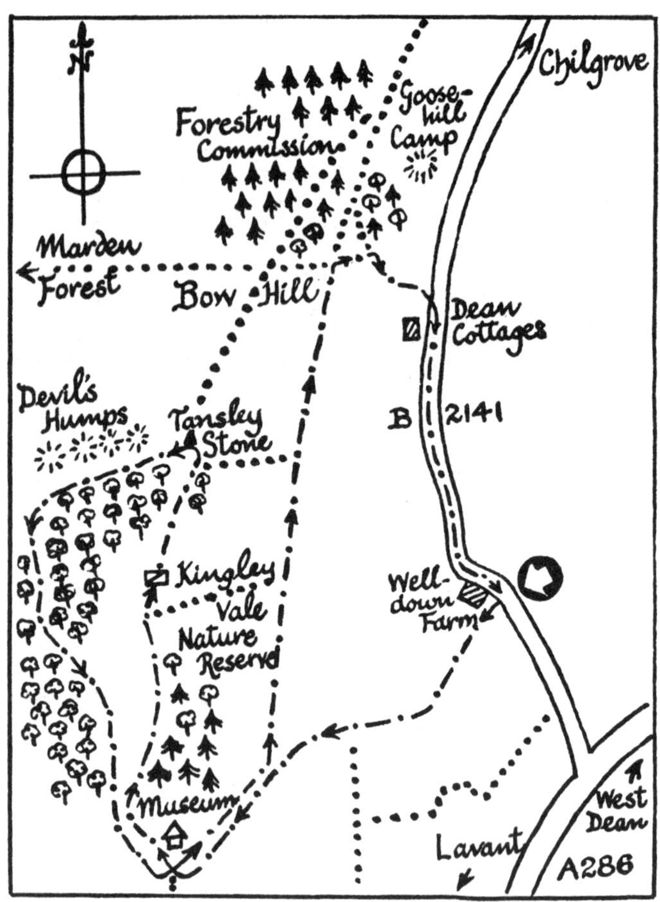

Walk 3

planted to commemorate a battle won by the men of Chichester against Viking marauders in AD 859; others say that King Alfred defeated the Danes here – hence, *King*ley Vale. Up on the skyline you will see the profiles of tumuli known as the Devil's Humps.

Soon you come to a point where a fingerpost points four ways; you will return here but meanwhile carry straight on.

The path descends between high hedges and at the next junction you will come to a notice-board created by the Nature Conservancy, displaying a map of the Kingley Vale Nature Reserve. Study it well, and get your bearings.

On your right stands a small wooden pavilion; this is a museum that, in the summer months, displays exhibits of the plant and animal life that abounds in this protected area of chalk downland.

Take the path to the north and, extracting a leaflet (there is a small charge) from its box, follow the numbered posts around the reserve. Reading from the most interesting leaflet, your attention will be drawn to the nature of the soil, the grasses, shrubs and trees, the seventy species of birds, and the deer and other animals that are encouraged to thrive in these 350 acres of woodland protected from the destructive hand of man.

This area is said to be the finest natural yew forest in Europe; many of the trees are from three hundred to five hundred years old and in even earlier times it is reputed to have been a Druids' grove.

At the corner of the woods, leave the numbered posts behind, and mount a stile and climb up across a paddock north to a copse and, passing through this, the path turns left (past some old flint mines) along the escarpment of the down. You will see what appears to be a sarsen stone, but it bears a bronze plate stating that it was erected in 1957 to the memory of Sir Arthur George Tansley FRS, founder of the reserve. The view from here is magnificent. You can see the coastal plain with the numerous inlets of Chichester Harbour and, on clear days, as far as the Isle of Wight.

The path now leads up to the Devil's Humps. These are tumuli – burial mounds dating back 3,500 years to the Bronze Age. Climb to the highest one and you will look down on to the villages of Walderton, Stoughton, West Marden and across the plain to Petersfield.

Proceeding on past the marked posts of the nature reserve your way is downhill, through copses and between high turf banks – all of which have some particular interest – and so back to the little museum.

Go back along the track by which you approached Kingley Vale until you come to the four-way fingerpost previously mentioned. Turn left along a path between broad flat fields; when you have passed them you will be climbing the southern slopes of Bow Hill (how could it be named otherwise, with all these yew trees?).

The path leads up to a pleasantly wide ride with Forestry Commission plantations on the left and, after a mile or so, you come to the earthworks known as Goosehill Camp. Turn back along the path curving down to the south; this will bring you back again on to the B2141. You can then walk back along the pleasantly wide grass verge, past Dean Cottages and Crows Hill Farm, to the point where you started – Welldown Farm.

---

4. The Trundle, West Dean, Colworth Down and Singleton Open Air Museum

This is a somewhat strenuous eight-mile walk and this mileage does not include the visit to the Weald and Downland Open Air Museum at Singleton, but the route can be shortened to suit the stamina of the walkers; your dog will enjoy it. Refer to OS map sheet SU81.

Start off at Goodwood, at the foot of the hill known as The Trundle. On the east you will see the famous racecourse and its grandstand, but set off westward, where you will find a signpost pointing the way up the steep hill.

The Trundle (or Hoop) is said to have been built up in the early Iron Age – about 600 BC. Its clearly defined ramparts enclose an area of about twelve acres. Stone-age pottery was found on the site by archaeologists, as well as the bones of oxen, sheep and pigs, revealing that the site was occupied four thousand years ago, but the iron-using Celts built up the hilltop fortress in its present configuration; it is considered to have been one of the largest and strongest forts in this part of England.

Leaving The Trundle, your path goes due west, crossing a narrow road and along the southern boundary of West Dean Park. You will come to a pleasant, white-fronted, flint-walled house and, about six hundred yards past this, your path veers north-west through Calhouns Plantation and downhill for about a mile to the village of West Dean. Cross the little bridge over the river Lavant and go along the lane to the main A286 road.

You can refresh yourself at the Selsey Arms. The inn sign appears somewhat unusual in heraldry – two ladies in evening dress, complete with ostrich plumes, appear to be supporters for the coat of arms.

Cross over the main road and go up the lane beside the schoolhouse. You will pass under an old railway viaduct and then this most pleasant lane leads upwards through a beautiful wooded valley, with Whitedown Plantation on your left and Warren Hanger on your right. There are public paths

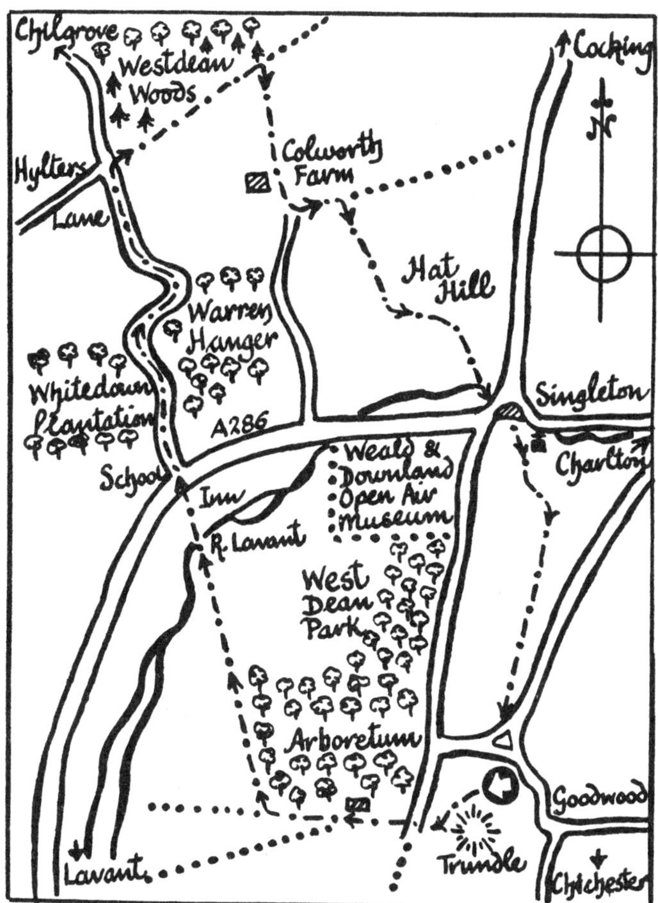

Walk 4

through the woods but the lane is generally quiet and easy for walking.

The lane rises for about two miles towards Colworth Down, where you meet Hylter's Lane and turn north-east, skirting Westdean Woods for about half a mile. Then take the path on the right, going due south to Colworth Farm. Past the farm buildings you will find yourself on a metalled road. Turn to the east here for about 150 yards until you come to some sheds; opposite these is a fingerpost by a stile, pointing to a path that goes south-east over Hat Hill and down to Singleton. This is a glorious walk, with grand views of the wooded hills of West Dean, Singleton Forest and Charlton Forest.

Arriving back on the A286 at Singleton village, cross over and take the road south for a very short distance. Then, on your right, you will see the entrance to the Weald and Downland Open Air Museum. Here, many old timber-framed houses dating back to the Middle Ages, and condemned to be destroyed, have been rescued and carefully renovated and rebuilt by dedicated people, to form a living museum. You will find a tollhouse, a medieval cottage, a granary, an Elizabethan farmhouse and many other ancient edifices exactly as they existed and appeared in their various periods in time. In the woods of the beautiful parkland in which these buildings stand you will be able to see a Saxon weaver's hut, a charcoal-burner's camp and an ancient sawpit. A visit provides the unique experience of travelling back in time, and you can rest and picnic in the grounds before continuing your walk. The museum is open from Good Friday onwards (except Mondays).

On leaving the museum, cross over the road and go into Singleton village and visit the church. This dates back to 1001 and many parts of the Saxon structure are still existing. Inside, the pews are five hundred years old and there are some interesting tombs and a font, once locked to prevent witches stealing the holy water. In the churchyard is an epitaph to a famous local huntsman:

> Here Johnson lies. What hunter can deny
> Old Honest Tom the tribute of a sigh?
> Deaf is the ear that caught the opening sound
> Dumb is that tongue which cheered the hills around.

On the west of the churchyard is a very narrow path that leads into a farmyard. This can prove to be very muddy (due to the surfacing of an underground stream) but you must circumvent it and go due south beside the fence and up the very steep pastureland of Knight's Hill; you will arrive at the road that takes you back to the Trundle.

---

5. Halnaker Mill, Eartham, Selhurst Park, Stane Street and Boxgrove

This is an interesting ten-mile walk, shown on OS map sheets SU90 and SU91.

Going from Westhampnett on the Petworth road (A285),

about half a mile beyond Halnaker village, is Warehead Farm. Leaving the road at this point is a lane, between high banks, leading due north-east. At the end of the lane is a stile and a path heading a short distance due north to Halnaker Mill.

It is as well to make the steepish ascent to the mill at the start of the walk – while you are still feeling energetic; dogs

Walk 5

can be brought, but on some long stretches they must be kept on a lead because sheep and cattle are likely to be encountered several times.

The climb to the mill is rewarded with splendid views in all directions – on clear days the Isle of Wight is clearly visible. The windmill itself was in ruins for many years.

Hilaire Belloc wrote:

> Sally is gone, that was so kindly,
> Sally is gone from Ha'naker Mill
> And the briar grows, ever since then, so blindly
> And ever since then the clapper is still,
> And the sweeps have fallen from Ha'naker Mill.

But, in 1934, the genial squire of Eartham, Sir William Bird, restored the mill to its present condition – with its fixed sails – as a fitting memorial to his wife. Only a few years ago the mill languished in a jungle of undergrowth but, thanks to voluntary clearing work by students, it now stands in a pleasant green sward.

Return down the steep path to the stile and, near it, there is a fingerpost pointing north-east along a narrow path. Follow it and you will find yourself on a raised bank; this is the 'agger' of Stane Street, built by the Roman legions to connect Chichester (Regnum) with London. Below, on the right, is an undulating quarry, often used as a venue for clay-pigeon shooting.

Keep to the path, crossing fences by quaint but convenient iron step-ladders. Eventually, the path slopes down to meet the A285 road again at Seabeach Farm. Along the road, opposite the entrance to Selhurst Park, there is a marked path, but you must ignore this and stay on the straight main road for about half a mile until it bends sharply to the left (north).

Leave the road at this point, on the right-hand side where the fingerpost points north-east, and you will find yourself back on the original Stane Street again. As you follow the path, note that ancient yew trees are growing straight out of the crest of the agger. The path leads through the pleasant woodland of Bushy Copse and eventually emerges on to the Eartham–Upwaltham road, opposite the Forestry Commission car park.

Turn left and follow the road north-west for a few hundred yards, until you come to a fingerpost on the left, pointing due west, and take the path between an avenue of Scots firs; you will meet the A285 again, but cross straight over the road on to a wide track that leads across the broad farmland valley of Selhurst Park.

A few yards along the track, opposite a dry dew-pond, you will see a fingerpost on the right, pointing to a public path that leads north-west across pastureland until you come to a stile by a spinney and a four-way fingerpost; here you proceed almost due west through sparse woodland until you come to the Goodwood road.

At this point there is a post pointing to a path leading south, beside the dense woodland that rejoices in the name of Open Winkins.

At the time of writing, the path is subject to a temporary diversion but, either way, you eventually come to the same point on the route. Instead of entering Open Winkins the very broad ride passes between these woods and Red Copse and leads down past Lady's Winkins to Halnaker Park.

Soon, you come close to a high flint wall on your right and opposite some cottages is a rather impressive gateway to Home Farm. Do not go through the gate but continue walking along by this high wall; it is beautifully constructed with knapped flints and you will note that, between the courses, flint chippings are embedded in the mortar; this is known as galletting.

As you pass along by the huge, ancient oaks, look back to the left and see the ruined wall and arched entrance to what was once Halnaker House. It was the home of Thomas West, ninth Earl De la Warr, who surrendered it to Henry VIII in 1540. A new mansion now stands on the site.

Now, still beside the high flint wall, you come to Park Lane and exit through another splendid gateway on to the A285 again. Here you will see a welcome sight – the Anglesey Arms; while you are enjoying a well-earned drink you will observe, in a glass case, one of the most gargantuan freshwater fish to be caught in England – a stuffed pike that weighed no less than 45½ pounds when alive.

You should not leave this area without visiting the secluded Priory of Saint Mary and Saint Blaise – a short distance down the lane, at Boxgrove. It is all that remains of a vast Benedictine monastery that was reduced to a ruin at the Dissolution, but the church itself is still a place of worship and has particularly interesting architecture dating back to Norman times; the elegantly vaulted chancel roof is magnificent. An exquisitely sculpted and painted feature is the Tudor chantry tomb built for the above-mentioned Earl De la Warr – this chantry, with its Gothic and Renaissance details, is well worth the deviation from your route.

Returning to the A285 and turning right, you will soon come to the point where you started out – Warehead Farm.

6. Stane Street to Bignor Hill, Stammers and Eartham

This walk is approximately eight miles long and is also shown on OS map sheet SU91. It will take about 3½ hours.

The Romans built Stane Street to link the sea port of Chichester (Regnum) with London (Londinium); it passed through Pulborough, Billingshurst, Ockley, Dorking, Epsom, Merton and Tooting. We are indeed most fortunate in West Sussex to have a surviving stretch of the road in a condition approaching its original state. The first part of this walk covers the route along Stane Street from Eartham to Bignor Hill (dogs must be kept on a lead).

As shown on the map, the starting point is about a mile north of the George Inn at Eartham; there is a large car park adjoining the Forestry Commission's North Wood Plantation. You will see the notice giving details of interesting walks through the plantation, where various species of trees can be identified.

But our walk starts at the National Trust notice-board – which gives a brief description of Stane Street; we are told that it was in use as early as AD 70.

The Roman road goes, straight as an arrow, north-east – passing between thickly planted, gloomy plantations. The surface is metalled with flints and has a definite camber; it is laid on a raised agger and surface water drains into parallel ditches on either side. These excavations were probably made to obtain the flints for the road.

About a mile and a half along, you come to the end of the Forestry Commission's plantations and there is quite a meeting of footpaths and bridleways at this point; note it well, because you will be returning to this spot.

Once clear of the woodlands, the configuration of Stane Street stands out more distinctly. Passing through a wicket and a field gate, you will discover that the road continues on a high agger, with sloping green banks between it and the flinty arable fields on either side; it is not difficult to evoke the image of a Roman legion marching along this route.

The walk continues most pleasantly for another mile and then you will see the rooftops of Gumber Farm below you, on the right.

Stop here and look back – to take in one of the grandest views in Sussex. On a clear day you will see beyond Nore Hill and Halnaker windmill, the coastal plain spread out before you, and the Isle of Wight rising steeply from the sea. This area is The Gumber.

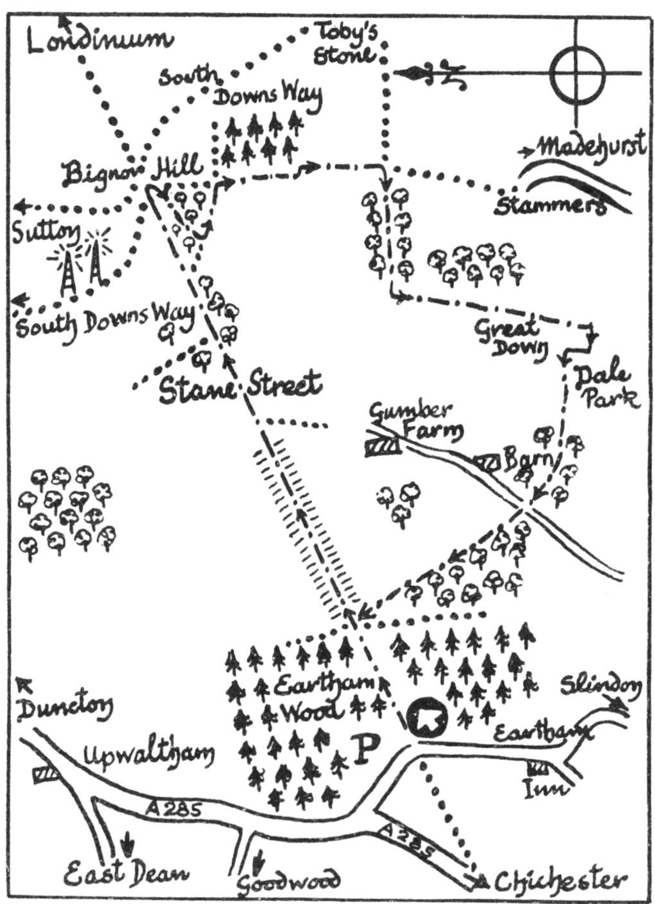

Walk 6

Hilaire Belloc, that great poet of the southlands, wrote:

Lift up your hearts in Gumber, laugh the Weald
And you, my mother of the valley of Arun, sing.
Here am I homeward from my wandering,
Here am I homeward and my heart is healed.
You, my companions whom the world has tired,
Come out and greet me. I have found a face

More beautiful than Gardens; more desired
Than boys in exile love their native place.

A mile past Gumber Farm, Stane Street leads on to heathland and, eventually, to Bignor Hill, where the signpost points from Regnum to Londinium. Rest on the grassy southern slopes and look down towards Sutton, and beyond that to Petworth and the broad landscape of the Weald. Just south of this point a smaller road branched off from Stane Street and led to the Roman villa at Bignor, the residence of the governor of Regnum.

Turning your back on the signpost, take the path leading south-west through the scrub and trees until it intersects with another path at the edge of the scrubland; turn left for about a hundred yards and you will come to a gate. Turn right, go through the gate and take the path leading almost due south; there is a wood of conifers on the left and arable land on the right. The path, going downhill, opens out to become a very broad way leading down to the lovely, secluded house called Stammers, but well before you reach the house you must take the first path to the right (west). This dips down to a pleasant little glade and then up through the trees; go straight ahead.

You will come to a fingerpost by a gate; turn left (due south) and walk across three broad fields of pastureland – Great Down. The path is not always clearly defined, but head due south through the gates on the further side of each field; you will again have a good view of Nore Hill and Halnaker windmill to the west.

At the third gate is another fingerpost. Turn right – to the west – and a short distance along is another fingerpost. This time turn right again – to the north – skirting a wood. Soon you will come to the point where the path forks; bear left, north-west, along the path through the trees and, where you reach the edge of the wood you will come to a flinty cart road leading to Warren Barn, but go straight across the road and continue along the path between fences. This is a pleasant, slow climb up into the Forestry Commission woods and you will soon return to the point where Stane Street leads back along the way you came from Eartham.

I consider this walk, with its historic interest, splendid views and diverse terrain, to be one of the finest in Sussex.

We are generally indebted to the Sussex Rights of Way Group for keeping the paths clear, but the stretch of Stane Street approaching Gumber Farm was nobly cleared by a commando group of the Ramblers' Association under the direction of an officer of the National Trust.

7. Sutton, Duncton, Tegleaze and Bignor Hill

This is an all-day walk covering about ten miles over the western Downs, and starting from the White Horse at Sutton; again, details are shown on OS map sheet SU91.

Right beside the pub car park is a path that passes between the houses; you go through three wicket gates – west, then north for a short distance. Reaching a stile, you will see a signpost pointing the way across a broad arable field to Barlavington; on your right are the church, rectory and houses of Sutton village. On the far side of the field you go down a steep, wooded dingle and across a footbridge over a pretty stream. All the time, you are heading north-west and fingerposts point the way to Barlavington Farm.

The public path goes left, around the western side of the farm buildings, and leads into the graveyard of the church of Saint Mary. This is a most interesting building dating from the twelfth century, but there is evidence that it was added to in the sixteenth and carefully renovated and partly rebuilt in the middle of the nineteenth century. A booklet is obtainable in the church.

Leaving the church, take the lane going due south-west between high banks and crab-apple trees; this leads out on to the very narrow winding road that leads back to Sutton. But you must turn right (north-west); it is well worth following the road for about a mile, if only to see the fine old half-timbered, pink-walled house on the left-hand side.

Soon after passing the road on the right (going to Petworth) and going west up the steep hill on A285, you come to a car park on the right which, by courtesy of the Rees Jeffreys Road Fund, provides a vantage point for a grand view of the Weald. This amenity has been augmented by the Automobile Association in providing a viewpoint in the form of a metal table on which are engraved leader lines radiating out towards points of interest in the middle distance and on the horizon.

Carry on up the hill to the bend of the road; here a path on the right leads up to a fingerpost pointing the way south up a wide chalk lane between high banks. On the right is the Duncton chalk quarry and soon you will see the trees of the Bishop's Ring, a well-known landmark.

The path curves around to the west; do not be tempted to bear round to the right, but carry straight on over the downland turf and soon you will come to a very handsome signpost, marked with the names of the Cowdray Hunt and the

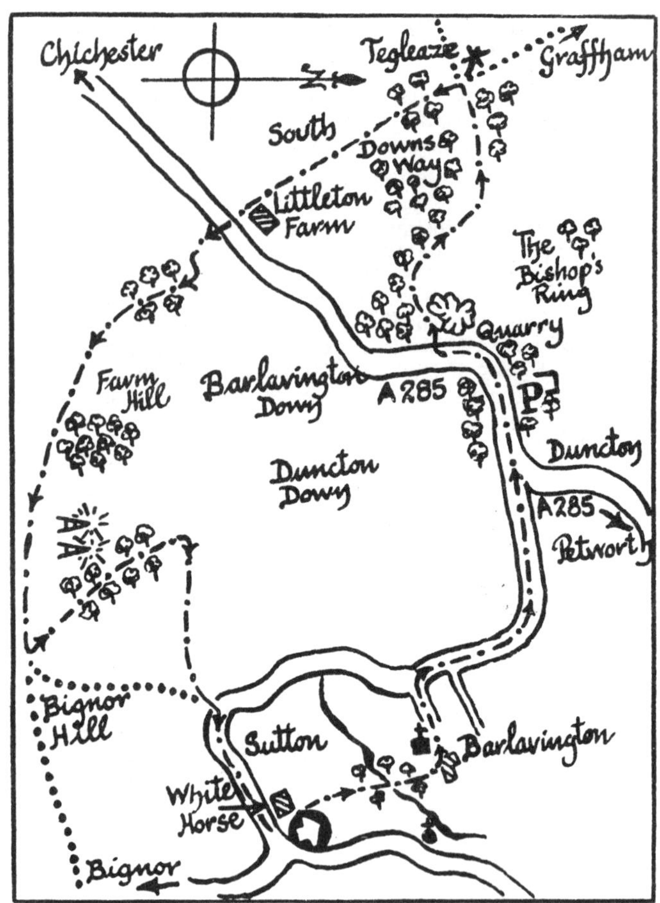

Walk 7

initials of other benevolent people who caused the post to be erected on its stone cairn. This is Tegleaze – the highest point on the western South Downs, about 837 feet above sea level.

The sign marks the route of the South Downs Way and here you turn sharp left along it and head south-east through the trees bordering Stickingspit Bottom. Emerging from the wood, your way goes downhill across broad arable fields to Littleton Farm on the A285. Cross over the road and, still on the South Downs Way, the path goes uphill – making a dog-leg – and due south-east across Littleton End; looking to the north you have a fine view of Duncton Down and Farm Hill.

The way goes across arable land and pasture, through a field gate and downhill towards private woodland, which you skirt on your left, and then uphill to the open downland. Here, you get the benefit of splendid views south-west across the coastal plain. Go along the path, still south-east, between arable fields and you will see the tall radio masts on your left. Soon you come out on to open downland again and will note that you have joined company with Stane Street – on its raised agger – and so on to the 'Roman' signpost on Bignor Hill. The extensive views from this point need no further description.

Now, you turn back north-west down the path shown on the sketch, then north-east; you will see Coldharbour and Glatting farms to the east. The path eventually comes out on the road back to the White Horse at Sutton.

---

8. Burton Park Lakes

This is a walk of about six miles through pleasant heathland and woods, with some particularly grand views of the landscape. It should take about three hours; your dog will enjoy it also – but must be kept on a lead towards the end of the walk; OS map sheets TQ01 and SU91 give details.

Going from Bury Gate, on the Petworth Road (B2138), and approaching Fittleworth, you come to a turning on the left leading to Coates; this is just before reaching the bridge over the river Rother.

A short way along this road, on the right, is the tiny church of Saint Agatha; this dates from the eleventh century and is well worth a visit; it possesses one of the few remaining square fonts in Sussex.

The road twists and turns past some picturesque old stone-built houses and, where the heathland of Sutton Common begins, you will come to a large, red-brick lodge on the left; here is a notice-board erected by the Barlavington Estate, welcoming visitors – with some reasonable reservations.

Just past the lodge, on the left, is a fingerposted path leading south-west through the woodland and sandy heath called Lord's Piece; you go straight across the Westburton road, skirting Broad Halfpenny and Column Hill, and come out by a farm at Sutton End. Here, you meet the road to Sutton, but turn right (due north) along it for about a quarter of a mile until you come to a fingerposted path under some tall trees on the left.

The post points along a gravel drive leading to the residence known as Sutton End; the lovely old-world garden of this house is open to visitors on certain days in the summer. Leave the drive just as it curves into the gateway and carry on along the path through Warren Woods, keeping the fence on your right. This is a very pleasant woodland walk for about half a mile; the path comes out on to the lane leading to Barlavington.

Turn left along the lane; you will see two small but interesting waterfalls bordered by ferns and cresses by the roadside and then, where the lane bends sharply to the left, Crouch Farm. This is a residence and, quite rightly, is marked private, but beside the gate is a fingerpost pointing north-west to a public path; note the interesting stone fountain beside the post.

The flinty path dips down between high sandy banks (the home of sand martins), then, emerging through the trees, you will come to the broad expanse of Chingford Pond. Here is one of the grandest views in West Sussex. Far across the shimmering, reed-bordered lake is the impressive background of the southern hills; you will see the heights of Duncton, Woolavington, Tegleaze and Graffham Downs, with the Bishop's Ring in the centre. The lake is a peaceful haven for waterfowl; in addition to the coots, moorhens and swans, you may catch a glimpse of the crested grebes as they surface between dives.

While you are admiring the lake, you will hear, behind you, the roar of a torrent. Quite close to the path, and visible over the low wire fence, on private land, is a most impressive waterfall. It was artificially contrived, but is more beautiful than many a natural one. The water from the lake, passing under the path, emerges foaming between mossy boulders and then cascades down to join Burton Mill Pond, which you will come to later on.

Continue along the path. On the left, in the distance, are the large buildings of Saint Michael's School, Burton Park, and on the right the riding stables. At the point where the path curves sharply left towards the school, the public path turns right (north-east) across heathland to the gate at the entrance to the private woods of Newpiece Moor; no horses are allowed in, and dogs should be kept on a lead.

On your right, you will get an occasional glimpse of the pond and, as you emerge from the trees, you pass through another gate on to a gravelled drive. This leads past the

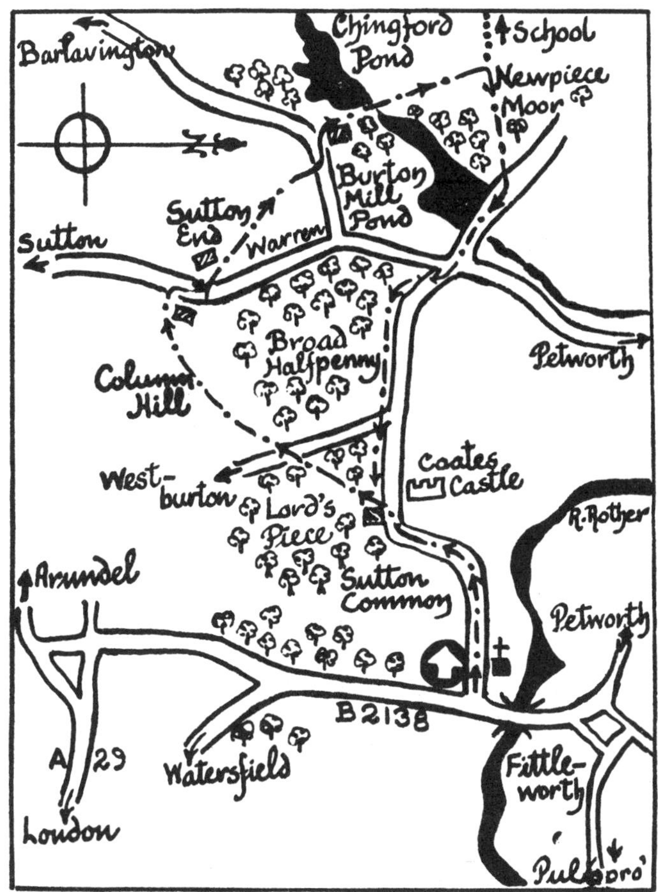

Walk 8

house and, at the large white gates, is the road back to Fittleworth.

Turn right here and you immediately come to the second wide and beautiful expanse of lake – Burton Mill Pond. Two fierce looking Muscovy ducks generally stand on guard on the roadside bank but, if you are patient, you are very likely to be rewarded with a close-hand view of more grebes.

Cross the road and look down on the roaring torrent of the millrace; the presence of all this water indicates that this locality is a major basin for the watershed of the South Downs.

Carry on along the road, uphill to the Sutton–Petworth crossroads, and go straight across. You do not have to walk on the road but can follow it on the grassy verges of Welch's Common and Broad Halfpenny. About a mile along, on the left, Coates Castle comes into view. This was once the home of the Duchess of Abercorn and also the Constable family. And so you return to the point where you started – on the road to Fittleworth.

9. Bury Hill to Bignor Hill and Westburton

This eight-mile walk, from Bury Hill to Bignor Hill, returning via Westburton Hill, is intended for vigorous and energetic participants because, towards the end, there is a very steep climb up the eastern face of the Downs. Cattle graze near to the unfenced footpaths, so dogs must be kept on a lead. The route is shown on OS map sheets TQ01 and SU91.

At the top of Bury Hill, where the trees have recently been felled and the road levels out, a fingerpost opposite Coombe Wood points the way west along the South Downs Way. Follow the track over the crest of the hill, pausing to look back at the hills and woods of Arundel Park and Amberley Mount beyond. When you come to the Forestry Commission plantation at Houghton Forest bear right by the fence, due north-west, and continue on along the gently undulating South Downs Way; excellent views of the woodlands extending south-west to Dale Park and Slindon are seen on this walk.

The track leads down to an intersection of paths; you cannot miss it because there is a high and capacious haybarn at this point, and the depression of an old dewpond on the right of the path. Here a fingerpost points the direction of the South Downs Way leading south-west up a steep hill, through scrub. Do not be tempted to take the level path, south across the fields to King's Buildings. Look back and admire the almost geometric curve of Westburton Hill.

Soon another signpost points a change of direction, at right angles, north-west, up the path to Toby's Stone. This is a mounting block erected in 1955 to mark the grave of James Wentworth-Fitzwilliam, a famous sportsman and Secretary of the Cowdray Hunt, who 'lies where he longed to be'.

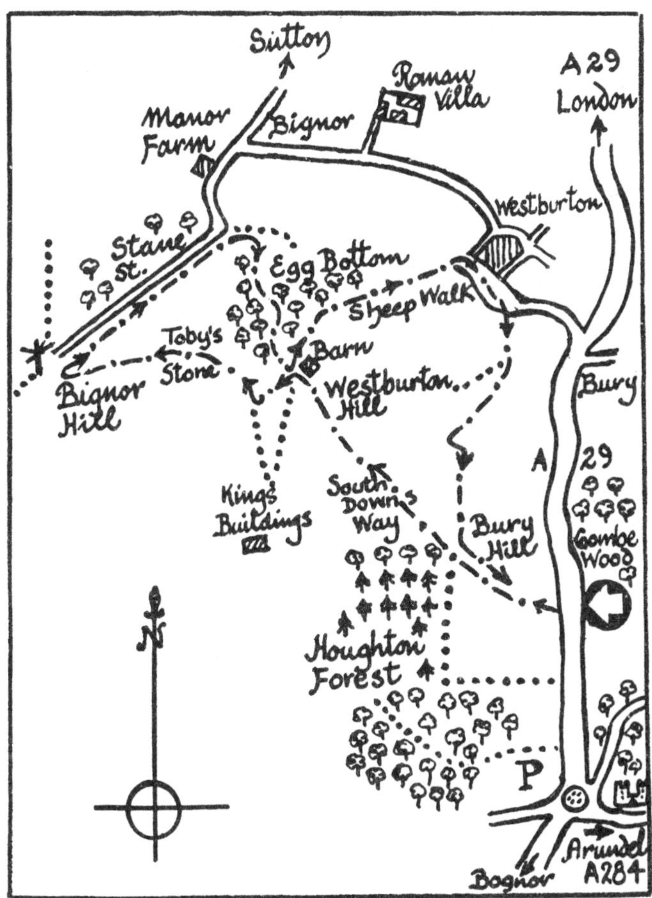

Walk 9

A few hundred yards further on you come to the crest of Bignor Hill and the large oaken signpost that points the way along Stane Street from Regnum to Londinium. You will want to pause and rest here to feast your eyes on one of the grandest views of the Downs and the great expanse of the Weald.

Follow Stane Street north-east, downward through the trees until you reach the sharp bend near the bottom of Bignor Hill, then leave the road and turn south-east along the wide flint path that skirts the rim of Egg Bottom Coppice until you come again to the great haybarn. Now turn sharp left, north-east, down the old sheep track that leads down to Westburton village. This is a beautiful part of the walk, between high green banks lined with oak, ash, hazel and the occasional yew; the writer has slept many a summer night under the trees here, to be awakened by the sound of the sheep bells as the shepherd led his flock to graze on the downland turf.

The path emerges between a house and cottage. Here you must turn right and follow the straight and narrow road along for some five hundred yards until it bends sharp left. Leave the road here and follow the fingerpost pointing to the path on the right. When you arrive at the fork be sure to bear *left.* The path is known locally as Poorgates Lane and, after a reasonably level start, it climbs very steeply through the beech hanger and up to the crest of Bury Hill.

Emerging from the trees, you cross a short piece of scrubland and pass through a fence to an arable field. Turn left along the edge of the field and, at the corner, you come to a path going due south between the fields; this path is bordered by a scrubby hedge and small trees and bushes.

You will eventually arrive back at the South Downs Way; turn left and back to your starting point.

---

10. Bury Hill, Coombe Wood and Houghton

A distance of about seven miles is covered in this walk, which begins on the A29 a few hundred yards north of the AA box at Whiteways Lodge. The route is shown on OS map sheets TQ00 and TQ01.

A fingerpost points to a path leading west towards Houghton Forest. The path turns sharp right and goes due north, along the edge of the Forestry Commission plantations. As you go along, look to the east, on the crown of the broad arable field, and you may see a small tumulus; this was the site of a windmill destroyed by fire in the last century.

About a mile along, after passing beside a blackthorn hedge, you will come upon the South Downs Way. Turn sharp right here and head eastwards, over the brow of Bury Hill; a fine view of Arundel Park can be seen to the south-east. Soon you will come back to the A29 again; cross over

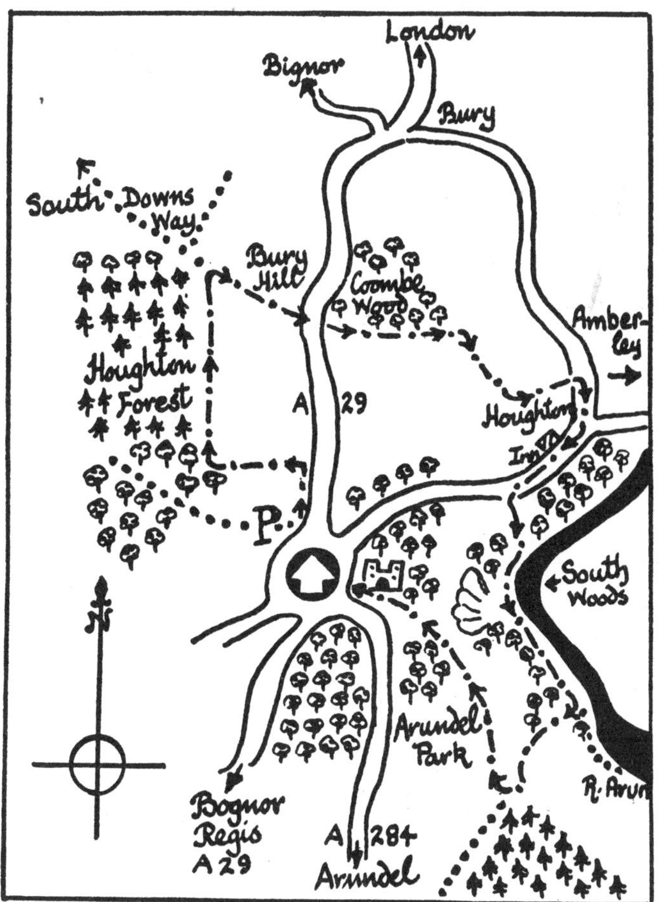

Walk 10

and go down the broad South Downs Way beside Coombe Wood.

After passing a flint-walled farmyard on your left, the view opens out and you get a splendid vista. Below, on the left, is the spire of Bury church, with the river winding past it; ahead are the Wild Brooks spreading to the walls of Amberley Castle. The river flows south, passing Amberley Mount and Houghton Bridge.

Your path turns south-east for a short distance and then, eastwards, descends steeply to meet the Bury–Houghton road. Turn right and walk up to meet the B2139 at Houghton village.

In 1292 the Earl of Arundel, who had been excommunicated for trespassing with his dogs in the Bishop of Chichester's forest, was received back into the Church at Houghton.

Turn right, and you will see the old, timber-framed George and Dragon inn nestling beside the road. Charles II paused here on his flight to the coast after the Battle of Worcester.

On leaving the George and Dragon, turn right and walk up the steep road for a short distance until you come to a fingerpost, on the left, pointing to a path that leads south-west beside a small paddock. Climb over the stile on the far side and you will find yourself at the top of a very steep Jacob's ladder. There is a handrail for most of the way to steady you on your descent through the trees to the river-bank.

The Arun flows quietly beside the broad green towpath and mirrors the small trees on its banks. On the far side the village of North Stoke is clearly seen against the background of the Downs. On your right the high and craggy chalk cliffs of South Woods are draped in greenery and below them is an amphitheatre of green turf – formed into little hummocks; this area was once reserved as a camping site for Boy Scouts.

Going south, you will come to the wall of Arundel Park. Houghton Lodge once stood here, but the entrance is now walled up. Between the wall and the river the path becomes quite narrow and muddy. Look out on the right for a break in the wall and a fingerpost pointing to a path that goes westwards. Now you will have quite a stiff climb, but pause to get your breath and look back across the river to the beautiful downland to the east.

Your path eventually leads up to a wire fence, where another fingerpost points south across Arundel Park. Do not follow this path any further. Turn right and go north-west along the broad path that leads up to Lonebeech Plantation. This is not a public right of way, but through the kindness of the Duke of Norfolk walkers are permitted to use this path back to Whiteways Lodge – provided that they do not bring dogs, cars or motorcycles into the park.

And so, after passing across the ancient earthworks known locally as the War Ditch, you will go out through the gateway of Whiteways Lodge to the point where you started.

11. Around Arundel Park

A quiet stroll around Arundel Park may be one of the easiest walks in the area, yet it affords some of the finest views of downland and weald that can be imagined. The distance covered is only three miles and is detailed on OS map sheets TQ00 and TQ01.

There is, in fact, only one public right of way across the park but, through the courtesy of His Grace the Duke of Norfolk, visitors may enter and walk around provided that no dogs, motorcycles or cars are brought in.

Start off by entering Park Lodge gate into Arundel Park. The lodge is at the end of a drive leading off the London Road as you leave the northern end of Arundel. There is a notice at the gate, referring to firing practice, but this is virtually out of date.

You will find yourself on a private metalled road leading to Whiteways Lodge. It is near the site of the old London road, and this fact emphasises that the park, as we see it now, has been completely encircled by the high flint wall only since the first decade of the nineteenth century, when Charles, eleventh Duke of Norfolk, enclosed the old London road within the park and provided the present one to replace it.

As you proceed north, the Hiorne Tower comes into view. This was named after the architect who built it as a mock-up for the Duke to approve the architectural style of the renovations to the castle between 1790 and 1810; the tower was lived in (it has circular rooms) until recent years, but is now uninhabited, being sadly vandalised. Beyond Hiorne Tower the ground slopes down Pugh Dene to Swanbourne Lake.

Looking back, across the other side of the road, you will be able to admire the elegant design of Arundel Park, the residence of Lavinia, Duchess of Norfolk. You will also appreciate the glorious view that opens up to the south.

The road passes between the wide, grassy practice gallops for the racehorses of the Norfolk stables. In pre-war years the area on the left was the site for the tents and picket lines of the Volunteers and later the Sussex and Surrey Yeomanry during their annual summer camps. Visitors to the park are asked to keep clear of these gallops.

Soon, looking north, you will see the chalk butts of the rifle range in the valley below Box Copse; then you will enter the trees of Park Rough, on the left, and Michael's Beeches on the right. Here are ordinary oaks, beeches and hazel underwood, but you will also see one or two Turkey oaks,

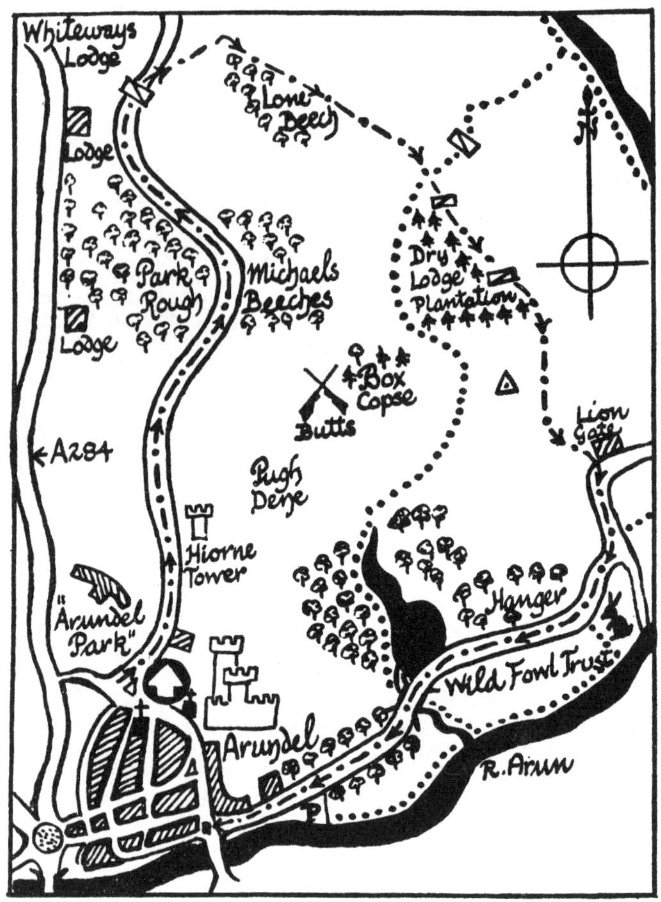

Walk 11

with their pointed leaf-lobes and hairy acorn cups. Notice the path on the left; this curves down to Green Lodge, hidden in the valley below.

Emerging from the woodland, you will find Duchess's Lodge on your left and, a few hundred yards on, the hard road ends at a white five-bar gate. As you turn, to close it after you, you will see a delightful view down the long, wooded valley to Swanbourne Lake. This is truly 'where the South Downs slope to meet the sea'.

Now bear slightly right; walk ahead through the thin line of Lonebeech Plantation. Suddenly, as you emerge through the trees on the escarpment, one of the finest views in England will present itself. Down below, the silvery river Arun curves past the high chalk cliffs of South Woods. To the east you will see North Stoke nestling in the valley, and Amberley Mount rising high behind it; beyond that are the beeches of Rackham Clump. Straight ahead, to the north, the broad plain of the Weald spreads out, and in the distance you will see the profile of the North Downs, near Guildford. To the west lies Bury Hill, and Westburton Down rises beyond it.

Turn sharp right, along the path that heads south-east, skirting Lonebeech; it widens out and becomes a broad track of springy downland turf. These wide, grassy tracks are typical of the South Downs but, unhappily, many were ploughed up during the Second World War.

Looking down, to the east, you will note South Stoke and Canada Farm above it; in the distance you may just discern Chanctonbury Ring. To the south, along the Arun Valley lie the lower slopes of the park – then, the coastal plain, and the sun glinting on the sea. Soon the path narrows and divides. The left-hand fork leads downhill to Blue Doors, but go through the gateway on to the right-hand track skirting the fir plantation on the site of Dry Lodge; far to the east, Highdown Hill can be seen on the skyline.

Passing through another gate, beyond the plantation the ground rises towards the concrete column of an Ordnance Survey triangulation point on the 350-foot contour level. Here you have a choice of two ways home; you can bear to the right and go down a pleasant valley past Shepherd's Garden to Swanbourne Lake, or you can descend the steep chalk path on the left down to Lion Gate – where Leo challenges the Fitzalan horse to leap across from one gatepost to the other.

Ahead leads the road to Foxes' Oven and Offham, but you will want to turn off it to the right and, possibly, pause at the Black Rabbit inn before proceeding past the Hanger to Swanbourne Lake, Mill Road and back to Arundel.

Allowing for long pauses to drink in the beauty of the downland scenery, the route from Park Lodge to Lion Gate will take about one and a half hours – say, two hours back to Arundel.

12. To Rackham Clump from Burpham

This route covers between seven and eight miles and is shown on OS map sheets TQ00 and TQ01. There will be cattle grazing, so the presence of a dog is inadvisable.

On this walk, from Burpham to Rackham Clump and Amberley Mount, returning via North Stoke, you always seem to be able to look ahead to the next objective, and there are fine views to be had at almost every point of the compass. Set off along the pleasant, straight road on the north-west side of Burpham church; to the west, the heights of Arundel Park and the castle can be seen and below them Offham and South Stoke.

When you reach Peppering Farm turn sharp right and follow the road uphill until you come to the T junction. Turn left (north) here and continue on to Peppering High Barn. Passing in front of the barn, follow the flint road as it curves round to the north-east. This is a splendid escarpment that gives impressive views across the wooded Arun valley to North and South Stoke and the Downs beyond.

After nearly a mile along this deeply rutted road, you will come to a triangular patch of scrub and small trees (a good place for blackberries in the autumn); this area is unusual in that electricity pylons have actually been removed from here. Follow the fence round to the right, north-east, until you come to a fingerpost on the left-hand side of the track indicating a public footpath through the trees. Follow this footpath until you reach the edge of the scrub, where another fingerpost is set beside a stile. Cross over the stile and follow the straight and narrow path north, beside the hedge between two fields; you will soon arrive at a broad flint track.

Turn right, east, and go to the end of the track, where it intersects with a straight path heading north-east. Turn left; the path passes between hedges but you will be able to look to the east and see the promontories of Wepham Down, Harrow Hill, Blackpatch Hill and, in the distance, Cissbury Ring; there is a tumulus near to the path, on the right.

Rackham Clump soon comes in view to the north, so you can keep it in sight until you reach gorse scrub; then your footpath bears left. You will pass a number of footpaths; these are among the many kept cleared by the voluntary workers of the Sussex Rights of Way Group. There used to be a number of small dwellings in Rackham Clump, occupied by a family of flint pickers, but their huts were used for target practice during the war.

You are now on the South Downs Way. Turn due west

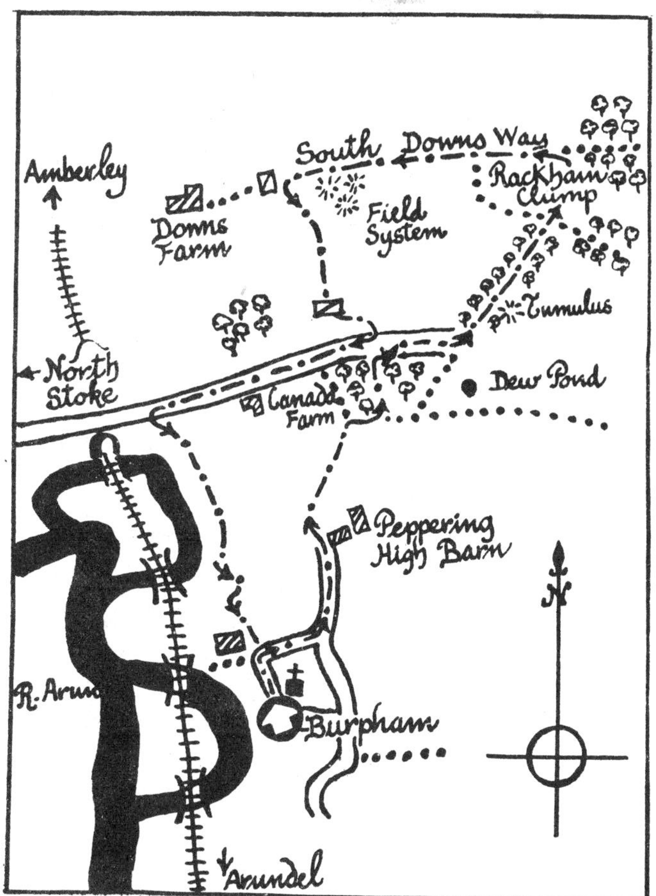

Walk 12

along the broad and level ridgeway, looking north across the Weald to see Parham Park and Amberley Wild Brooks, with the whole western range of the Downs as a magnificent background. This is an invigorating, slightly downhill walk all the way to Amberley Mount, and it is steeped in prehistory. You will pass tumuli and neolithic earthworks and, to the south, a Celtic field system; there is also one of those ancient 'green roads' that were once arterial thoroughfares.

Descending Amberley Mount, you will see Downs Farm ahead, but before reaching it, you pass through a field gate. Turn due south here, along a fingerposted path, going steeply downhill towards Stoke Hazel Wood; at the bottom of the valley, which is generally swampy, pass through a fence and a gate and climb the very steep path curving south-west to the west of the hill. Here you will meet a fairly wide flint track; turn to the right (west) and follow it until it becomes a road passing the barns and byres of Canada Farm.

Now you will see on the left the escarpment along which you came from Peppering High Barn. Follow the road downhill until you nearly reach North Stoke. On the left, above the entrance to the main-line railway tunnel, there is a fingerpost pointing down south-east towards the river valley. Descend the green path to the old course of the river Arun and follow its bank until the railway comes in sight. Turn due south-east here, along a straight path across the water meadows until you reach the trees. Here, the path leads back to Peppering Farm and so back to Burpham.

---

13. Parham Post to Chantry Post via Lee Farm and Harrow Hill

This downland walk covers between five and six miles and is detailed on OS map sheet TQ01.

You can drive up or climb the steep road to Parham Post. Take the road from Amberley to Storrington (B2139) and, about two-thirds of the way along, turn right – past Springhead Farm – up a narrow lane, with a hairpin bend, that leads to the crest of the Downs. Leave the car here.

Look northwards and you will see, beyond the demesne of Parham House, Northpark Wood, Wiggonholt Common and the plain of the Weald stretching away to the North Downs.

Look south and, if the day is reasonably clear, you will see the Isle of Wight rising from the sea. To the west is Rackham Clump, with the South Downs Way leading up to it.

Walk straight across the Way, where the white post points to Burpham. Then descend into a little valley, with scrubland on your right and a broad field on the left.

At this point I must warn you not to bring your dog. On the gates, which you must pass through, is a grim notice to the effect that cavorting canines will be executed on sight. You are entering sheep country! But to those of us who

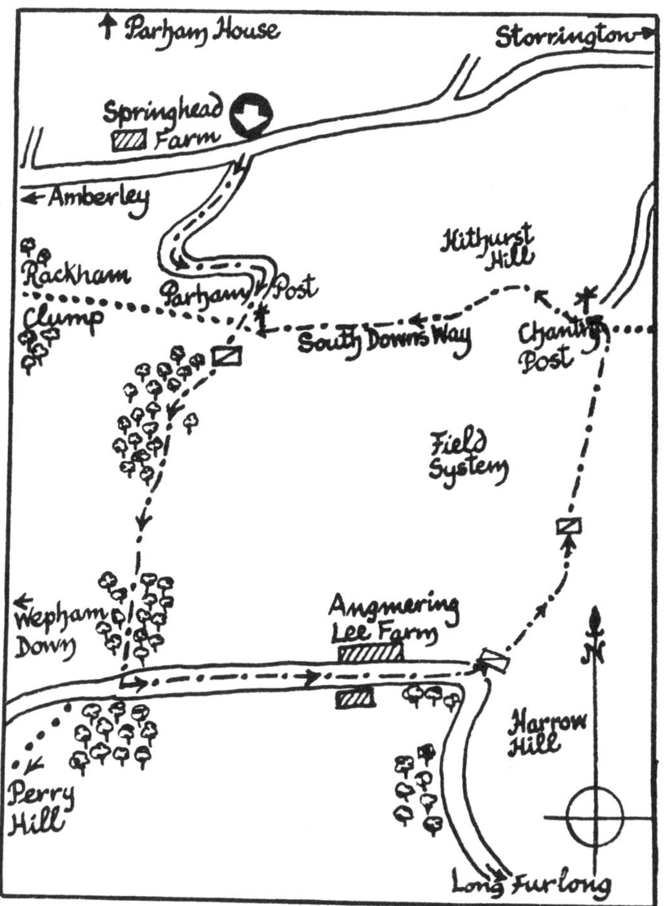

Walk 13

remember the clanging of their little bells in pre-war years, it is a great joy to see the flocks returning to the Downs.

The wood, on your right, is particularly prolific in bird life, at appropriate seasons; sparrowhawks abound and they hunt the predatory pigeons. On the vast acreage of arable land on your left Roman remains have been found in the past.

When you leave the shelter of the trees the view to the south-west opens up to reveal the escarpment of Perry Hill, curving away towards Burpham. You can also see the Arun valley, with Arundel Castle and park away to the west.

Now, for a short distance, the path becomes a muddy lane through a rather dismal, silent wood – but once out of it you come to a T junction with a farm road. Turn sharp left here; the road passes between the large, modern buildings of Lee Farm, headquarters of the agricultural activities of the Duke of Norfolk's estate.

But the road is, in fact, a public bridleway, as you will see from the signpost as you leave the farm.

Right before you, to the east, tower the neolithic fort and flint mines of Harrow Hill – but the Romans were there also. A local downsman, 'Skipper' Phillips, found, in a rabbit-hole, half the base of a Samian-ware cup; he returned a year later to find that the furry archaeologist had obligingly excavated the other half!

The farm road now bears to the south but, at the bend, leave the road and pass through a gate on your left (another dog warning): follow the path as it curves northwards. Soon you will come to another gate and, at this point, a splendid view opens up to the east.

Here you will be able to appreciate the majesty of Harrow Hill, with Blackpatch Hill (more flint mines) beyond, and beyond that the earthen fortifications of Cissbury Ring. To the north-east you will see the trees crowning Washington Bostel.

In this quiet and generally lonely area of bare downland you are truly in the home of our early ancestors. As you continue on the path as it rises towards Chantry Hill, you can clearly see, on your left, the low embankments that marked the boundaries of a Celtic field system.

It is rather a long, slow haul up to Chantry Post, but when you get there you will find seats by the white signpost that points to Amberley, Storrington, Washington and Lee Farm. Rest here and enjoy the expansive view of the Weald below you.

Then you can take the South Downs Way to the west. Rackham Clump is ahead, but you are not going so far; you will return to your starting point at Parham Post. On the north is Kithurst Hill, the site of a neolithic pottery, but your path traverses the south side of the escarpment – so you will be enjoying the sight of the valleys leading down to the sea.

It is a pleasant walk, but not so enjoyable in certain conditions. On foggy nights, in the times when the paths led to thriving downland villages, wayfarers could be lost. It is said that one such benighted horseman, the local rector, was lost in the fog; he could not tell if he was facing south, or the dangerously precipitous north. He had the presence of mind to bark like a dog – and the dogs answered him from the farms far below, at the northern foot of the Downs.

14. Pulborough, Stopham and Hardham

This is a relatively short walk of five miles, but there are so many places of interest en route to visit, that it could well occupy an entire morning or afternoon; the route is shown on OS map sheet TQ01.

Going north, cross over the river bridge at Pulborough and go up the short steep hill on the road to London. At the crest of the hill is the ancient lychgate to Pulborough church, but before passing through it, look back across the main road and see the fifteenth-century cottage perched high on the sandstone rock of the embankment. This cottage, with its frame of oaken timbers, is reputed to conceal deep cellars in the sandstone where smugglers once stored their booty.

Now go up the steps and through the lychgate to the church of Saint Mary, which crowns the hill at Pulborough; its square tower, with its battlements, can be seen from a great distance. This church was mainly built during the first forty years of the fifteenth century, from stone quarried locally; full details of the architecture and monuments, etc, are given in the booklet obtainable in the church. There are some splendid tombs and also brass portraits on the walls, which are of great interest to the visitor.

Leave the church by the path leading from the north porch, and go down into the narrow lane that leads westward. Turn left, passing a group of fairly modern houses, and, crossing a railway bridge, you will come to a narrow lane going due north. At the corner, on the right, is Old Place – some say it was once a priory, and the mellow old stone walls do convey this impression; clearly, the walls of this gracious house show evidence of arched entrances filled in, and later Tudor window openings formed.

Beyond the house is a vast fishpond, once renowned for its carp. The pond was channelled to drive the huge waterwheel of the ancient mill on the left of the lane – now a private house. Now turn back to the road by which you came from the church and turn right along it. This narrow road winds between borders of hazel and small trees and then, on your left, you will see a green-painted sign pointing to a path that runs due west beside a wire fence across the fields. Halfway along, you will have an unrivalled view of the northern escarpment of the South Downs; over to the east is Kithurst Hill, then Parham Post, then, ahead, Rackham Clump, and so on, westwards, to Amberley Mount.

At the end of the path is a modern piece of fortification – a concrete strongpoint. This is in a very strategic position as it commands a wide field of fire over the river valley, to the south. Passing the picturesque old buildings of Park Farm on your left, go straight on south-westward, to the path that leads into Pulborough Park plantation. Note here the great variety of species of young trees on your left. Spruce, larch and maple grow alongside the birch, oak and ash. This is a very pleasant walk, with sandy heathland to the north and the grand vista to the south across the Arun valley to the Downs.

Soon you come in sight of Cheal's Nurseries, on the left; then, further on, to your right, you get a most unusual view of the narrow Arun, below you, winding its way northward through water meadows. The path ends, most conveniently, outside the door of an inviting grey stone inn, the White Hart. Go up the steps and into the snug old bar, with its ancient inglenook.

Duly fortified for the next stage of the walk, cross over Stopham Bridge and admire its singular beauty. This is one of the most visually pleasing bridges in the south-east of England. It was built in the fourteenth century and has a high-arched span in the centre – with three lower ones on each side. The piers are buttressed with projecting cutwaters, and there are recesses on the parapet for the refuge of pedestrians – a truly beautiful bridge, but one that suffers sadly from the impact of heavy modern traffic.

From the crown of the bridge you will catch a glimpse of Stopham House, the ancestral home of the Barttelot family, who have been here since the Norman conquest; it is said that at one time they could ride from Stopham to Horsham without leaving the bounds of their own domain. They are a family with a great military history that continues into the present generation, but Stopham House now comprises a very comfortable home for the elderly people of the county.

Go back over the bridge and along the A283 for a short distance east towards Pulborough. Then, on your right, you will see a sign pointing south towards the river – which you will cross by a narrow footbridge. The waterways become most interesting at this point. At the bend where the Arun turns north, you will clearly see the opening of the old Western Rother Navigation canal that, between 1794 and 1885, flowed from here to Midhurst.

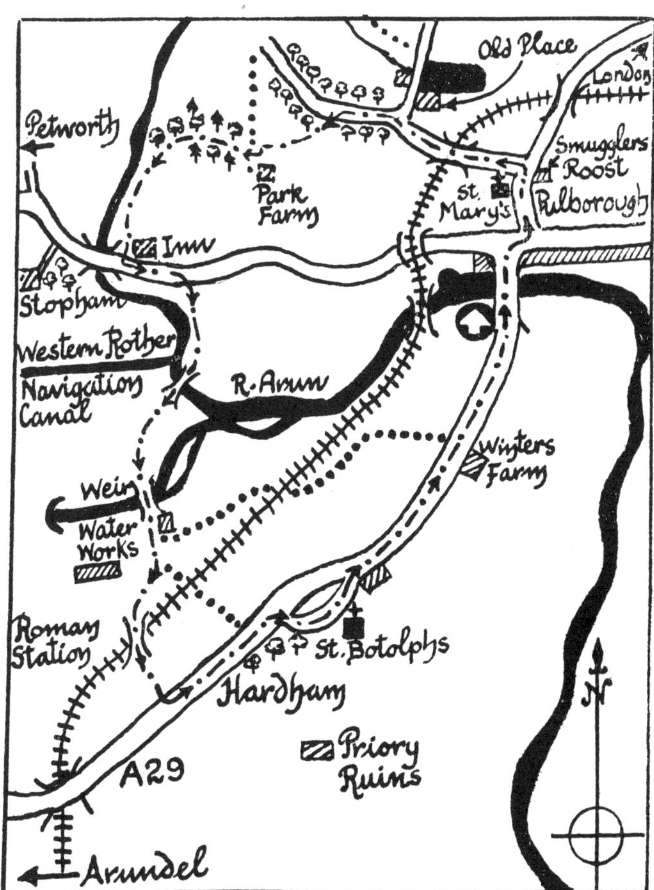

Walk 14

Continuing south-west across the fields, you will arrive at a most interesting weir and a waterway that once connected the Arun to the Rother. The channel ran through an underground tunnel, but this is no longer navigable. At the centre of the weir, you will note two rectangular concrete tanks at two levels; these form a 'ladder' by which the trout can leap over the weir on their journey upstream. This water was stocked with fish by the Sussex River Authority, whose large complex of buildings houses the water-treatment plant on the site of old Hardham Mill.

When you come abeam of these modern buildings, take the path leading south-west across the fields; this path crosses over the old, disused Fittleworth railway line, and goes on to a bridge that crosses the existing main line to the south. Pause on the bridge and look westward; this is the site of the old Roman staging post on Stane Street – the first stop between Regnum and Londinium.

Cross over the main road and look across the fields in a south-westerly direction. You will see the ruins of the Augustinian priory of the Exaltation of the Holy Cross, founded about 1250. The ruins may only be visited by permission of the owner, who lives in the adjoining house.

Now walk along beside the A29 going north-east towards Pulborough. About half a mile along you will see, on the right, the tiny little church of Saint Botolph. This you must visit; the church 'is unique in its possession of the earliest, nearly complete, series of wall paintings in the country. They date from shortly after 1100'; so states the leaflet obtainable in the church. This is a splendid little publication, because it not only gives details of the church, but also the origins of Hardham and the priory.

Leaving the church, you will only have a mile to go along the road to Pulborough Bridge.

---

15. Blackpatch Hill, Chantry Post, Harrow Hill and Myrtle Grove

A downland walk of nearly seven miles is described here and detailed on OS map sheets TQ00 and TQ01.

The sites of neolithic flint mines in Sussex are on the summits of the hills; consequently, visits to these areas are rewarded with commanding views of downland scenery.

The reason for the high location of the mines is that the most prolific sources of suitable flints for implement-making were found in the upper chalk strata. Up on these hills, it is easy to evoke a picture of the activities of the neolithic men. The miners passed up the flints to the surface, where the craftsmen sat on the sunny slopes and knapped the stones into the required shapes – flakes of these flints are still to be found. The complete story is excellently presented in visual form at Worthing Museum; this walk passes near two of the sites (see sketch-map).

The road from Clapham to Findon (A280) forms a right-angled turn to the east at the approach to Long Furlong.

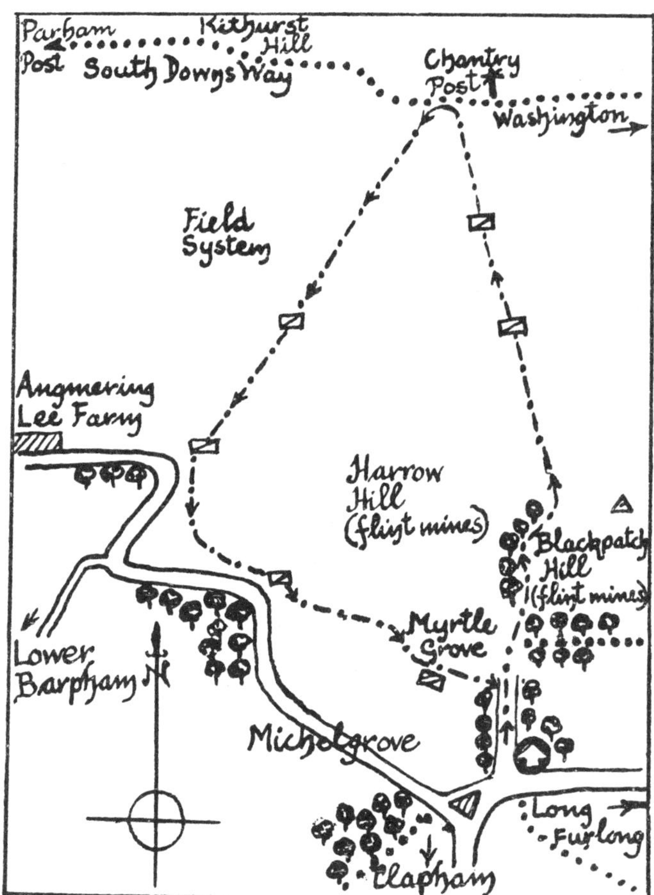

Walk 15

Take the lane going due north from the bend in the road, Longfurlong Lane. This is a gradual climb between arable fields to Blackpatch Hill, 555 feet above sea level. Approaching the summit, note the interesting lines of stunted beeches forming wind-breaks on the hillside. Looking south, between the trees, you will see the farm buildings of Myrtle Grove and, on the skyline, Highdown Hill.

The path skirts the south-western side of Blackpatch and then goes dead straight north-west – descending past a steep valley on the left. Harrow Hill, also on the left, rises to almost the same height as Blackpatch. Look out for a tumulus on the left of the path and pause at this point to appreciate the view to the south-east, where the grassy ramparts of Cissbury Ring form the horizon, with the slopes of Middle Brow and Church Hill intervening; a Romano-British settlement was sited to the north of the latter. Looking out to the west, the heights of Perry Hill and Wepham Down are to be seen; Rackham Clump is on the north-western skyline, with Kithurst Hill to the right of it.

Carry on along the path and proceed up to Chantry Post; here you can rest on a seat and look out across the broad landscape of the Weald – in clear weather even as far as the North Downs.

Turn back again down the broad track – south towards Harrow Hill. Look out on your right to see the low, angular embankments that formed the boundaries of Celtic farmers' fields. Soon you will sight the modern complex of agricultural buildings that comprise Angmering Lee Farm (note the warning sign that dogs must be kept on a lead). Do not go through the gate and on to the farm road, but turn due south along the path that first runs parallel to the road; the path passes over the south-western slopes of Harrow Hill.

The path curves down over the brow, to meet the farm road again, but here, at the wicket gate, you will come to a fingerpost that points the way south-east along the public path to Myrtle Grove. Ask permission to pass between the farm buildings and take the road, still going south-east, to meet Longfurlong Lane again.

---

16. Clapham, Long Furlong and Patching Hill

The pleasures of downland scenery, woodland walks and visits to ancient churches are all embraced in this seven-mile walk. Details are shown on OS map sheet TQ00. There are fair stretches where dogs may run free, but they will need to be led through game woods and, in the Forestry Commission areas, there is a warning that vermin traps are set. The walk takes about 3½ hours.

Opposite where the road from Angmering meets the A27, by the Horse and Groom hotel, take the lane leading north to Patching village.

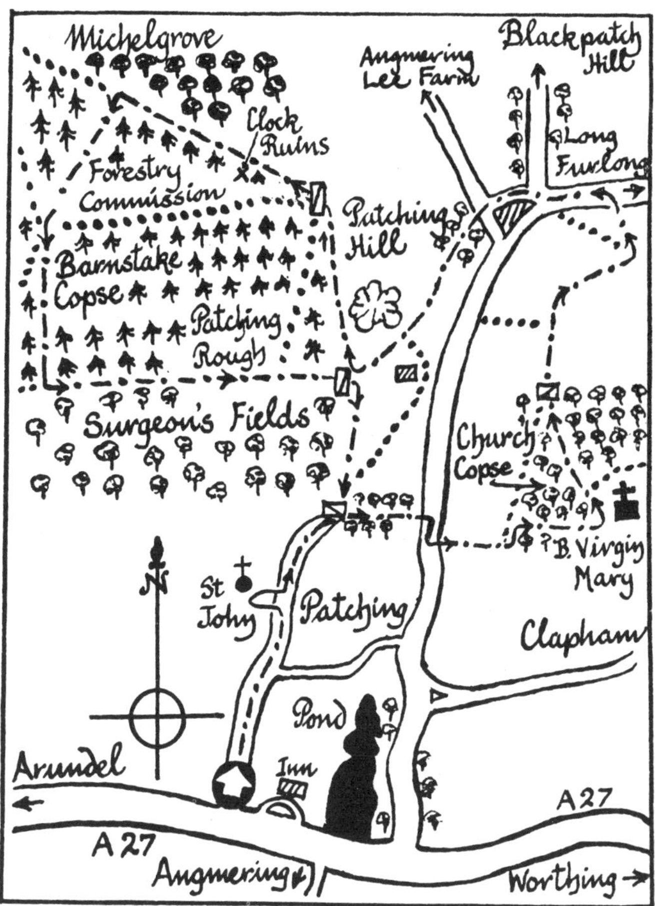

Walk 16

You will soon see the church of Saint John the Divine. This building, with its elegant spire, is certainly worth visiting. It has Saxon origins, having been given to Canterbury by Wilfric in 948, and it has been conserved and restored right up to the present day by the benefaction of local squires. A booklet obtainable in the church gives the story not only of the church but also the history of Patching village as a whole.

Leaving the church, carry on up the winding lane until it is closed by a rail fence. Turn right to face a field gate, but do not go through it; look for the half-concealed path to the right. Go down the narrow path between high, ivy-covered banks under overhanging trees – proceeding south-east. Emerging from the trees, the path passes between broad arable fields and ends at the road going almost due north towards Findon.

Turn right and follow the road for a very short distance – until you come to a fingerpost pointing to a path on the left. This path will lead you uphill across a meadow and, after crossing two stiles, you will find yourself on a path leading into Church Copse. Be sure to bear round to the right, through the hazel underwood, until you come out opposite the church of the Blessed Virgin Mary, at Clapham. Look over the low flint wall ahead of you; the half-timbered farmhouse of mellow red brick and its setting amid the paddocks and cottages evokes memories of a bygone age – but do not go down the lane to the right unless you are interested in modern villas.

Parts of the beautiful flint-walled church date from the twelfth century and improvements were added during every successive century; extensive restoration was carried out in the 1870s under the direction of Sir Gilbert Scott. Here again the booklet obtainable in the church gives a great deal of historic information on the parish, with particular reference to the famous Shelley family of Michelgrove.

When you come out of the church turn right and follow the fingerposted path north through the private game woods of Goring Hall Estate; do not be tempted to follow the broad track curving to the right (east). At the end of the wood you come to a kissing gate that opens on to a broad, sloping meadow. Go straight across and over the stile on the far side. From here you can see splendid views of Chanctonbury Ring.

Your path curves to the right over green downland and then down a sharp descent to the left – on to the Long Furlong road. Your booklets will tell you that this was built in 1818 as a coaching road, to curve in a broad sweep across the Downs from Clapham to Findon.

Turn sharp left, due west, along the road for a short distance. When you come to the sharp bend you will see a fingerpost pointing south-west to pass behind the romantic turrets of a pumping station; considerably more crude solutions might have been found for the architectural problem of fitting this functional edifice into the downland scene.

Crossing the lane that goes to Lee Farm and Michelgrove, the path goes uphill through a leafy tunnel for a short distance and then a gate opens on to the broad green slopes of Patching Hill. Walk up the clearly defined ramped path that curves round to the west – on the right of the reservoir.

Pause by the gate at the top. Here is one of the finest viewpoints in West Sussex. To the south – beyond the green spire of Patching church – Highdown Hill can clearly be seen on the skyline, and over the treetops of the dense woods the sea seems quite near. To the north you will see the Long Furlong valley and Chanctonbury Ring beyond it, while to the north-west the humps of Blackpatch and Harrow hills loom high in the landscape. On the summits of both these hills shafts were sunk by neolithic men to mine flints.

When you follow the fingerposted path due north-west, you will find that some saintly person has provided a seat on which you can rest and enjoy the grand prospect of the Downs. Having rested, walk on along the path going due north-west towards the woods. On the way, you will notice on your right the track of an ancient path that led to Michelgrove Park; sometimes this track is on a raised agger and sometimes it descends between high green banks – there is also the declivity of an old dewpond on the right.

You enter the Forestry Commission woodlands through a gate and will no doubt be pleased to note that these plantations are not gloomy, regimented rows of conifers but are of deciduous trees – oak, ash and beech. The path passes between some posts but go straight on, north-west, past two fingerposts. You will pass close by a heap of rubble; this is the ruin of a clock-tower erected by a Mr Walker, who acquired the Michelgrove estate from the Shelleys; it is said that the clock itself was eventually installed in the tower in Steyning High Street.

Turn left at the point shown on the sketch and take the path that goes due south for a mile; then you will arrive at a wide and well-worn main track running east. Follow this right to the end of the woodlands and you will emerge on to a path running between broad fields of arable land; you will then arrive back at the gate on Patching Hill. Turn right, downhill to the lane that leads back through Patching village.

---

17. Chanctonbury Ring

You will cover about seven miles on this walk, which is shown on OS map sheet TQ11. It will take about three hours, and your dog will enjoy the run.

Chanctonbury's hill, crowned with its ring of beeches standing out on the skyline, is probably the most dominant feature in the West Sussex landscape; its north face is precipitous.

There are numerous paths leading to the summit: a long and easy ascent from Findon; a steady climb from Washington; a level approach from Cissbury or from Steyning Round Hill, and there is a steep climb from near Wiston. But the object is to walk a circular route with the most attractive scenery.

So, start at Steyning and walk down the High Street (A283) in a westerly direction until it turns sharp right towards Washington; but you walk straight on along the narrow, quaintly named Mouse Lane. Passing between high banks, the lane leads to Charlton Court, on the right.

Opposite the entrance you will see a signposted cart track leading south-west. Continue up this track, with a hedge on the left and arable land on the right. The track becomes a footpath as you walk up it. Pause and look back at the beauty of the Weald, then carry on until you enter a wood; here the path forks, but continue straight on. Emerging from the wood you look down to the south, across the lovely valley of Pepperscombe, east to Steyning Round Hill and beyond that the northward-jutting green promontories of Beeding Hill, Truleigh Hill, Newtimber and Woolstonbury – one of the finest views of the South Downs.

The path, entering a spinney, gets steeper here and it forks, but keep to the main (wider) section. Still climbing you bear right; there is a high, wooded bank on the left and on the right you look down into a valley where there is, or was, a rifle range. Suddenly you emerge on to the bare down, or rather arable land. Turn sharp right along the bottom edge of the field, with Court Plantation on your right. Continue on until you come to a fingerpost directing you to turn left. You will pass along the western headland of the same field, slowly climbing, until you reach the broad track of the South Downs Way.

Now, to the west, you will at last see Chanctonbury Ring. Your way is easy now, up and down gentle slopes along the Way, above Lion Bank, until you reach the Ring; to the north, you will see below you Wiston House, a gracious Tudor mansion, its lovely lake and park. A Roman guardhouse was unearthed here in 1848.

As with almost every one of the South Downs, Chanctonbury was originally a neolithic camp. Flint implements have been found here and coins that prove that the Romans also appreciated the commanding military value of this site; it is

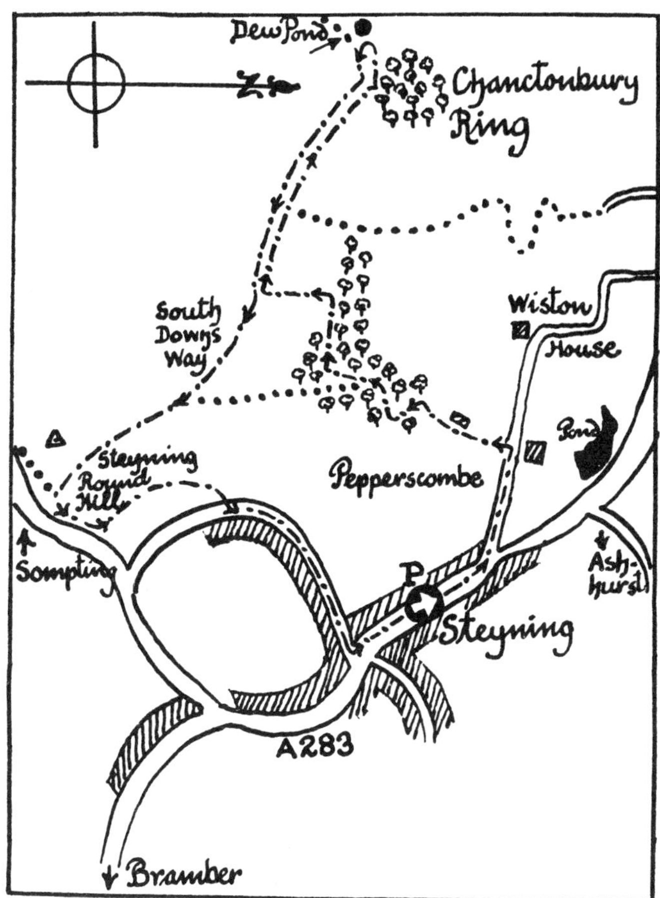

Walk 17

also rumoured that the Devil himself uses this as a trysting place with his devotees! The beeches and other trees were planted by Charles Goring in 1760; it is sad to learn that their days may be numbered.

Make your way around to the northern edge of the ring and just sit there and take in the majestic prospect spread out below you – the breathtaking beauty of the Wealden plain. When, at last, you have drunk your fill, continue around the trees till you meet the path to Findon and, just beyond a gate, you will discover a dewpond; in 1970–1 this was cleared and made wholesome by the efforts of the Society of Sussex Downsmen.

Turn back and return east about two miles along the South Downs Way. You will be rewarded with glorious views down the valleys of Buddington Bottom and Stump Bottom to the sea and, ahead, you will see the vallum crowning Cissbury Ring. Soon after passing a concrete OS triangulation point you will come to a stony track; turn left to Steyning Round Hill, with the Sompting road at its foot. Circle west around the Round Hill, until you see below you a straight path leading down; follow this north-east to Steyning, and back along the High Street.

---

18. Cissbury Ring

This route covers about 7½ miles and is shown on OS map sheet TQ10. Dogs must be kept on a lead near the gallops and also where cattle and sheep may be grazing.

Before visiting Cissbury Ring it is well worthwhile to call at Worthing Corporation Museum to see the excellent contour map of the site and the flint and metal implements and pottery discovered at this prehistoric settlement, which bring to life the day-to-day existence of its neolithic and iron-age peoples.

This imposing hillfort, with its tiers of ridged ramparts, rises to a height of over six hundred feet; it is at the junction of three chalk ridges extending from the south and south-east and is 3½ miles from the sea. On clear days the line of the south coast, from Beachy Head to the Isle of Wight, is visible from the summit. The following route has been planned so that the majesty of Cissbury Ring can be viewed from a number of different directions.

Set off from Findon at the point marked on the sketch-map and follow the road around to the left to Nepcote Green. At the annual county sheep market every square foot of this green is occupied by the animals – a sight worth seeing.

Turn to the right, east, and just past the last house in the lane is a fingerposted path leading north-east. This is a steady climb for nearly a mile, and on your right you will have a good view of Cissbury, looming high over Findon. Your path is bordered on the left by the gallops of the famous Findon

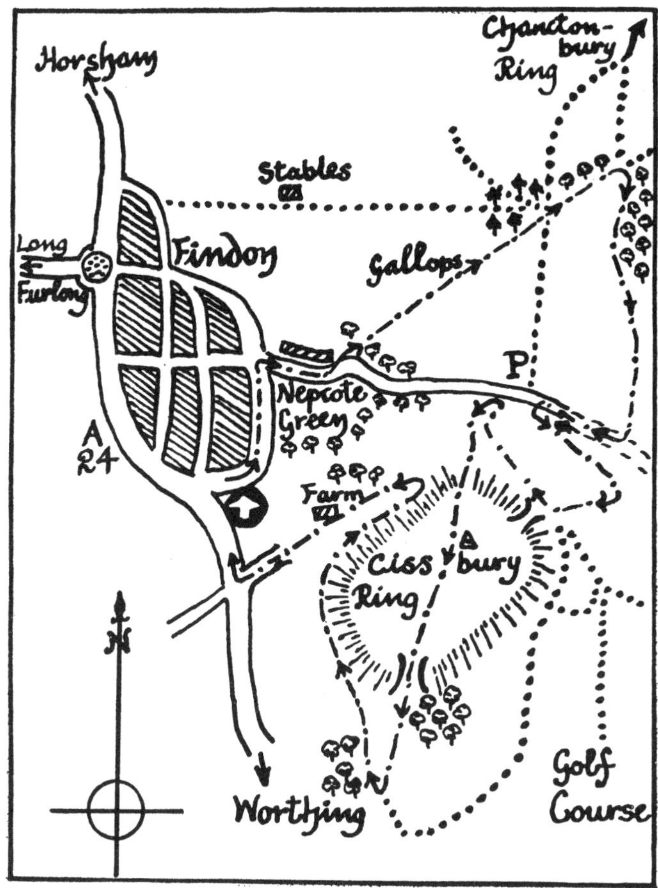

Walk 18

Stables and you are quite likely to see racehorses being exercised.

At the top of the climb you pass through a small spinney of Scots firs and then arrive at a four-way fingerpost. Cross over the wide path and go straight on. Here is a wide and unbroken prospect of rolling downland, with a fine view of

Chanctonbury Ring marking the line of the northern escarpment; a number of iron-age remains have been excavated from the hills on your left. In pre-war days, before the Downs were ploughed up, it was possible to look down on the valleys and discern clusters of dark rings in the turf; these were the sites where huts had existed in prehistoric times, and the rings were clearly revealed on aerial photographs.

Just over a mile along the path, you arrive at Stump Bottom. Turn sharp right, southward, here and follow the path as it winds along the valley under Park Brow; iron-age, bronze-age and Roman remains have been found here, and a Celtic field system existed on the east side – you will be truly walking through a cross-section of English history.

The path comes out at a flinty, rutted road. Turn right, due west, and walk up the road – with Cissbury Ring towering on the left. You will come to a solitary farm building on your left and will see a fingerpost pointing southward; follow the steep, chalky path up between the thorn-bushes and climb up to the Ring.

You will come to a National Trust signpost standing beside the entrance cut through the steep and massive ramparts of the fort. But do not go through this entrance; turn right and walk down the north-westerly ramp to the bottom of the hill, because here you will find a post bearing an excellent description of the history of Cissbury Ring and, in identifying the various points of interest, you will enjoy your visit the more.

You will note that although the sixty-five acres contained within the earthworks have been acquired for the nation by the National Trust, the site is managed by Worthing Corporation. Between 3000 and 2000 BC neolithic man dug shafts and horizontal galleries to mine the flints which they dug out using picks made from the antlers and shoulderblades of deer. The flints were passed up to the surface, where skilled craftsmen knapped them into shape and polished them to form weapons and domestic implements. They came to realise that the mined flints produced better artefacts than those found on the surface.

Climb up the steep path to the plateau at the top of the hill. The contours of the fort, as we now see them, were mainly the work of iron-age men, 250 to 50 BC. They built up a chain of these hilltop strongholds along the south of England – generally with ramparts forming a defensive enclosure for the plateau, where they and their cattle could take refuge. Cissbury is vaguely reminiscent of Maiden Castle in Dorset – but on a considerably reduced scale. In Roman times British farmers occupied Cissbury and later the Saxons came there.

Carry on along the path running due south across the plateau; you will see the OS triangulation point at 602 feet on your left. Pass through the southern exit through the ramparts and along a stony path beside Cissbury Plantation – a metal signpost points the way. The descent is very gradual, across the fields to another signpost by some trees to the south.

Here you turn back, north-west, along a gently descending path from which you can look up at the impressive southern ramparts of the fort. The path curves to the north, where you meet another path going back in the opposite direction, south-west – back past Cissbury Farm to Findon.

19. Edburton to Truleigh Hill, Small Dole and Tottington Sands

This seven-mile walk over downland and Weald takes about three hours. The appropriate OS map is sheet TQ21/31.

Between Upper Beeding and Poynings, turning east from the A2037 (Henfield) road, is the small village of Edburton. Go eastward through the village and turning due south from the road is a green bridleway that will take you by a steepish climb to the top of Edburton Hill.

Here you will come to a fingerpost – and another one beyond it. Go over the crest of the hill and through a gate opening on to a farm road that curves away to the south-west; this is, in fact, the South Downs Way. The coastline from Brighton to Worthing is clearly visible and, to the west, the promontories of the Downs.

Press on westward along the undulating track and you will very soon come to the television mast beside the barn on Truleigh Hill. The Downs at this point are more than seven hundred feet above sea level; consequently there is a particularly fine prospect, to the west, of Chanctonbury and Cissbury Rings.

Passing Freshcombe Lodge on the left, and Tottington Barn on the right, you arrive at a rather splendid and capacious youth hostel of functional yet pleasing design. This hostel is sited at an exceptionally good vantage point and is partially screened by Scots firs which form a short avenue along the South Downs Way.

A short distance along the Way turn right on to a path that leads due north across the Downs towards Tottington Mount. Then it veers left, to the north-west, and goes down to the road by which you travelled to Edburton. Turn right, along the road for a very short distance until you arrive at

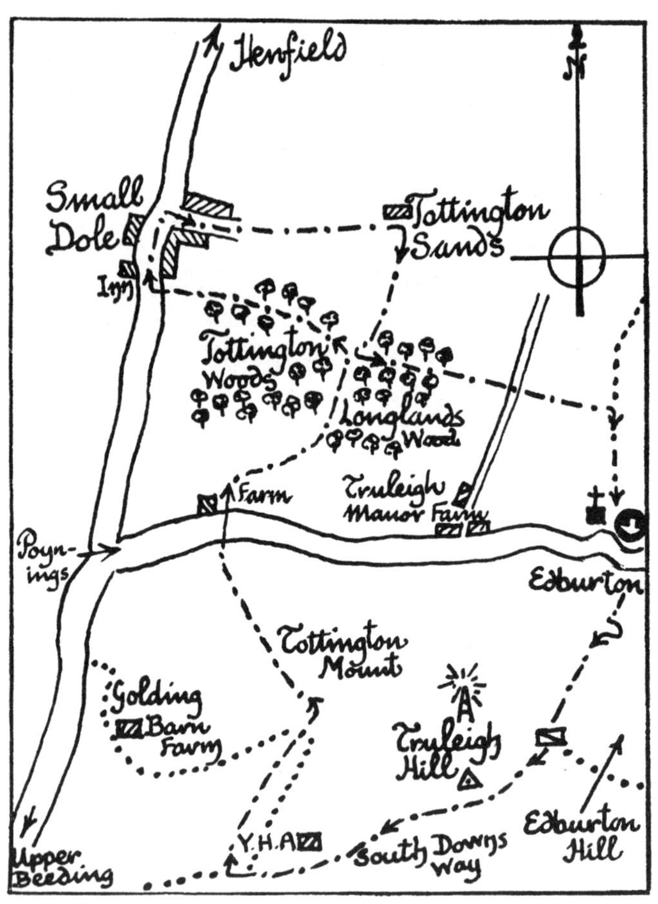

Walk 19

Tottington Manor Farm. Ask permission to go through the farmyard to the public path leading north to Tottington Manor Cottages; you will notice a warning that dogs must be kept on a lead.

The path leads into the green depths of Longlands Wood. You must keep to the path and will eventually arrive at a fingerposted four-way crossing (to which you will ultimately return). Turn left here, westward, into Tottington Wood. This path winds through the trees until you are going north again; there is some swampy ground on the right and, behind the trees on the left, a large factory. Then you come out on to the recreation ground at Small Dole.

Behind the western goal posts is a very short public footpath that brings you out on to the main road – with the welcome sign of the Fox and Hounds opposite. On the assumption that you have rested here, carry on along the main street of Small Dole in the direction of Henfield, then take the first turning right (by a telephone box).

This short road tapers off into a public footpath which goes eastward between the fields to the large farm at Tottington Sands. The path curves to the right, in a southerly direction; it is interesting to note that flint implements of the mesolithic period were discovered here. Leaving the farm behind you and keeping to the path, you will cross over a small stream and on to Tottington Woods again – where you will arrive back at the four-way fingerpost.

Now turn left, to the south-east, and passing through the cool glades of Longlands Wood you will emerge on to open farmland. Note the fingerpost pointing to the public path (still going south-east) along the edge of an arable field; at the end of the field the path joins a metalled farm road. Go straight across the road and continue on until you meet a path going south; follow this and you will arrive back at Edburton.

---

20. Perching Hill to Devil's Dyke, Poynings and Fulking

This five-mile route is shown on OS map sheet TQ21/31. You will probably encounter sheep and cattle grazing on the Downs and, since the return route follows the road, it would not be advisable to take a dog.

Eastward from Chanctonbury Ring the Downs are not cloaked with trees as in western Sussex; they begin to show the characteristics of the eastern hills that range to Eastbourne. Yet their very bareness has its visual attraction; their steepness and height appear more impressive and the sweeping curvature of the terrain is more emphasised.

To start, travel east from Steyning on A283; turn north on to A2037 beyond Bramber but then be sure to take the first turning on the right, marked 'Poynings' – the road runs along the foot of the Downs. About a mile past Edburton you cannot miss seeing a double row of electric power pylons; leave the road here and take to the chalk track heading due south. Passing through a gate, you will find that the path veers to the west and climbs across the steep northern face of Perching Hill. As you pause to take a breather, you will look out on to the broad chequerboard of the Weald.

At the top of the hill is the South Downs Way; follow it eastward along the crest of Fulking Hill. Looking seaward, the built-up coastline of Portslade and Hove lies below, and you cannot fail to note the cement works at Beeding, from which, recently, the single-span bridge was launched to carry the South Downs Way over the Adur at Annington.

Ahead of you, the earthen ramparts of an iron-age hill-fort are clearly discernible. Make towards the concrete plinth of an Ordnance Survey triangulation point but pass just south of it. Cross straight over the road that leads to the hotel but, before you reach the golf clubhouse bear left; this path traverses the top of the south-eastern bank of the Devil's Dyke, which is soon revealed.

This fearsome sharp and deep cleft into the Downs is most impressive and its origin must have puzzled people from time immemorial. The legend is that the Devil became furious because of the proliferation of Christian churches in the Weald and longed to drown them all, but the Downs formed an impregnable barrier against the sea. So he determined to dig a great ditch right through the hills and thus cause the plain to be flooded by the inrush of the sea. However, Saint Dunstan was able to thwart him by specifying that the Dyke must be completely finished by the dawn of the day after it was started. Then, with divine co-operation, the crafty saint caused all the thousands of cocks in Sussex to crow an hour early, so the Devil had to stop his digging. The most lively version of this legend is recounted by Hilaire Belloc in 'The Four Men'.

Your path very gradually descends along the length of the Dyke, north-east through the small thorn-bushes until, suddenly sloping more steeply, it reaches the bottom of the valley. Carry straight on through the trees, crossing a small pool and then passing a pond on your left, and you will soon find yourself at the very doors of the church of the Holy Trinity at Poynings; the vicarage behind the church is a charming building. The pond is reputed to be haunted: a drowning tragedy occurred there in 1883.

The name of the village and the history of the church devolves from the lords of the manor, the de Ponyngges family, one of whom, Michael, was appointed Guardian of the Sussex Coast in 1351. The family was held in royal es-

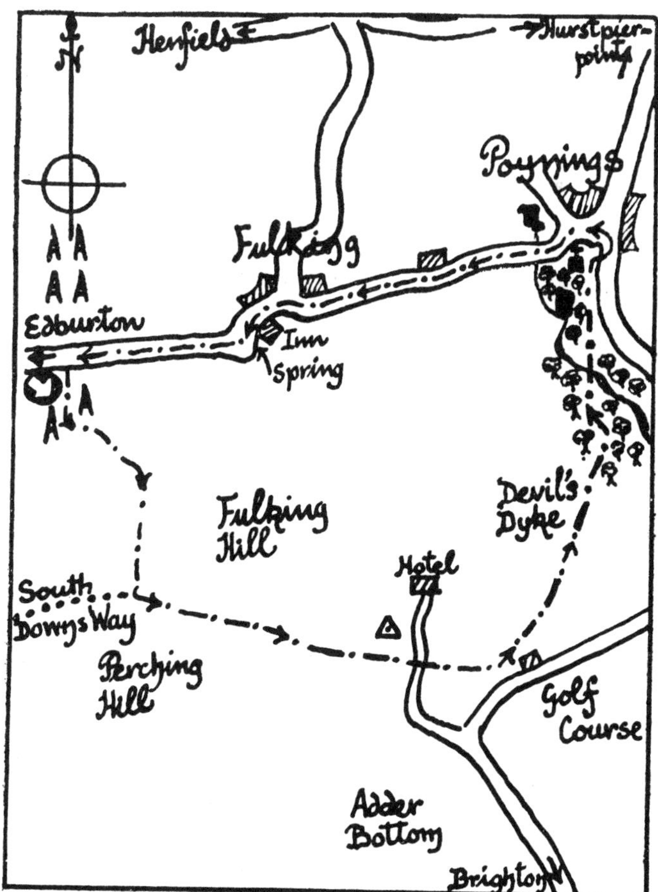

Walk 20

teem; it was in Poynings that Anne of Cleves found hospitality.

Leaving Poynings, take the quiet and narrow road west; it is an agreeable walk, on the grass verge, with the impressive heights of the Downs to be admired on the left and a well-preserved old flint building, Wickhurst Barn, on the right.

You will soon come to Fulking, a picturesque village with some notable specimens of timber-framed, thatched houses and cottages. The road, with an elevated footway beside it, goes uphill through the village and then descends steeply to the corner, where stands the ancient Shepherd and Dog inn – an indication of the dependence of this area on sheep farming.

John Ruskin, who often stayed at Fulking, admired the glorious sunsets over the Downs. Just beside the inn a spring, in the words of Esther Meynell, 'comes leaping out of the chalk with a shout!' The clear water is retained in a stone sink, beside which stands a small pumping station that bears a stone tablet, erected by the villagers to the memory of John Ruskin.

Continue along the road and you will very soon reach the point where you started this walk.

Index

Titles in the 'Discovering' series with their series numbers

Discovering Abbeys and Priories (57)
Discovering Antique Maps (98)
Discovering Archaeology in Denmark (141)
Discovering Archaeology in England and Wales (46)
Discovering Backgammon (201)
Discovering Backpacking (256)
Discovering Banknotes (146)
Discovering Battlefields of England (176)
Discovering Beekeeping (226)
Discovering Bells and Bellringing (29)
Discovering Bird Courtship (236)
Discovering Bird Song (202)
Discovering Brasses and Brassrubbing (9)
Discovering British Cavalry Regiments (157)
Discovering British Ponies (219)
Discovering the Burns Country (220)
Discovering Carts and Wagons (87)
Discovering Castle Combe (5)
Discovering Castles in England and Wales (152)
Discovering Cathedrals (112)
Discovering Chapels and Meeting Houses (209)
Discovering Chess (221)
Discovering Christian Names (156)
Discovering Christmas Customs and Folklore (32)
Discovering Church Architecture (214)
Discovering Churches (137)
Discovering Church Furniture (69)
Discovering the Cinque Ports (237)
Discovering Corn Dollies (199)
Discovering Country Crafts (230)
Discovering Country Walks in North London (240)
Discovering Country Winemaking (249)
Discovering Craft of the Inland Waterways (227)
Discovering Dowsing and Divining (251)
Discovering Ecology (154)
Discovering Edged Weapons (124)
Discovering Embroidery of the Nineteenth Century (99)
Discovering England's Trees (86)
Discovering English Architecture (244)
Discovering English Customs and Traditions (66)
Discovering English Dialects (235)
Discovering Epitaphs (144)
Discovering Essex (105)
Discovering Farmhouse Cheese (238)
Discovering Farm Livestock (246)
Discovering the Folklore and Customs of Love and Marriage (196)
Discovering the Folklore of Plants (74)
Discovering French and German Military Uniforms (186)
Discovering Gardens in Britain (56)
Discovering Geology (189)
Discovering Ghosts (147)
Discovering Hallmarks on English Silver (38)
Discovering Hampshire and the New Forest (60)
Discovering Harness and Saddlery (119)
Discovering Heraldry (250)
Discovering Herbs (89)
Discovering Horse Brasses (44)
Discovering Horse-drawn Carriages (194)
Discovering Horse-drawn Commercial Vehicles (224)
Discovering Horse-drawn Farm Machinery (245)
Discovering Horse-drawn Transport of the British Army (233)
Discovering Kings and Queens (151)
Discovering Lancashire (171)
Discovering Leicestershire and Rutland (82)
Discovering London Curiosities (165)
Discovering London for Children (110)
Discovering London's Guilds and Liveries (180)
Discovering London's Inns and Taverns (243)
Discovering London's Statues and Monuments (42)